EASY EVERYDAY DISHES

Consultant Editor
Bridget Jones

WARD LOCK

A WARD LOCK BOOK

First published in the UK 1994
by Ward Lock
Villiers House
41/47 Strand
LONDON
WC2N 5JE

A Cassell Imprint

Editor: Jenni Fleetwood
Designer: Anne Fisher
Cover artwork by Angela Barnes
Inside artwork by Kevin Jones Associates

Distributed in the United States
by Sterling Publishing Co., Inc.
387 Park Avenue South, New York, NY 10016-8810

Distributed in Australia
by Capricorn Link (Australia) Pty Ltd
P.O. Box 665, Lane Cove, NSW 2066

British Library Cataloguing in Publication Data
The CIP data for this book is available
upon application to the British Library

ISBN 0-7063-7182-8

Typeset by Litho Link Ltd, Welshpool, Powys, Wales
Printed and bound in Spain by Cronion S.A., Barcelona

CONTENTS

USEFUL WEIGHTS AND MEASURES

USING METRIC OR IMPERIAL MEASURES

Throughout the book, all weights and measures are given first in metric, then in Imperial. For example 100 g/4 oz, 150 ml/ ¼ pint or 15 ml/1 tbsp.

When following any of the recipes use either metric or Imperial – do not combine the two sets of measures as they are not interchangeable.

Weights The following chart lists some of the Metric/Imperial weights that are used in the recipes.

METRIC	IMPERIAL
15 g	½ oz
25 g	1 oz
50 g	2 oz
75 g	3 oz
100 g	4 oz
150 g	5 oz
175 g	6 oz
200 g	7 oz
225 g	8 oz
250 g	9 oz
275 g	10 oz
300 g	11 oz
350 g	12 oz
375 g	13 oz
400 g	14 oz
425 g	15 oz
450 g	1 lb
575 g	1¼ lb
675 g	1½ lb
800 g	1¾ lb
900 g	2 lb
1 kg	2¼ lb
1.4 kg	3 lb
1.6 kg	3½ lb
1.8 kg	4 lb
2.25 kg	5 lb

Liquid Measures Millilitres (ml), litres and fluid ounces (fl oz) or pints are used.

METRIC	IMPERIAL
50 ml	2 fl oz
125 ml	4 fl oz
150 ml	¼ pint
300 ml	½ pint
450 ml	¾ pint
600 ml	1 pint

Spoon Measures Both metric and Imperial equivalents are given for all spoon measures, expressed as millilitres and teaspoons (tsp) or tablespoons (tbsp).

All spoon measures refer to British standard measuring spoons and the quantities given are always for level spoons.

Do not use ordinary kitchen cutlery instead of proper measuring spoons as they will hold quite different quantities.

METRIC	IMPERIAL
1.25 ml	¼ tsp
2.5 ml	½ tsp
5 ml	1 tsp
15 ml	1 tbsp

Length All linear measures are expressed in millimetres (mm), centimetres (cm) or metres (m) and inches or feet. The following list gives examples of typical conversions.

METRIC	IMPERIAL
5 mm	¼ inch
1 cm	½ inch
2.5 cm	1 inch
5 cm	2 inches
15 cm	6 inches
30 cm	12 inches (1 foot)

OVEN TEMPERATURES

Three alternatives are used: degrees Celsius (°C), degrees Fahrenheit (°F) and gas. The settings given are for conventional ovens. If you have a fan oven, adjust the temperature according to the manufacturer's instructions.

°C	°F	GAS
110	225	¼
120	250	½
140	275	1
150	300	2
160	325	3
180	350	4
190	375	5
200	400	6
220	425	7
230	450	8
240	475	9

MICROWAVE INFORMATION

The information given is for microwave ovens rated at 650-700 watts.

The following terms have been used for the microwave settings: High, Medium, Defrost and Low. For each setting, the power input is as follows: High = 100% power, Medium = 50% power, Defrost = 30% power and Low = 20% power.

All microwave notes and timings are for guidance only: always read and follow the manufacturer's instructions for your particular appliance. Remember to avoid putting any metal in the microwave and never operate the microwave empty.

NOTES FOR AMERICAN READERS

In America the standard 8 oz cup measure is used. When translating pints, and fractions of pints, remember that the U.S. pint is equal to 16 fl oz or 2 cups, whereas the Imperial pint is 20 fl oz.

Equivalent metric/American measures

METRIC/IMPERIAL	AMERICAN
Weights	
450 g/1 lb butter or margarine	*2 cups (4 sticks)*
100 g/4 oz grated cheese	*1 cup*
450 g/1 lb flour	*4 cups*
450 g/1 lb granulated sugar	*2 cups*
450 g/1 lb icing sugar	*3½ cups confectioners' sugar*
200 g/7 oz raw long-grain rice	*1 cup*
100 g/4 oz cooked long-grain rice	*1 cup*
100 g/4 oz fresh white breadcrumbs	*2 cups*
Liquid Measures	
150 ml/¼ pint	*⅔ cup*
300 ml/½ pint	*1¼ cups*
450 ml/¾ pint	*2 cups*
600 ml/1 pint	*2½ cups*
900 ml/1½ pints	*3¾ cups*
1 litre/1¾ pints	*4 cups (2 U.S. pints)*

Terminology Some useful American equivalents or substitutes for British ingredients are listed below:

BRITISH	AMERICAN
aubergine	eggplant
bicarbonate of soda	baking soda
biscuits	cookies, crackers
broad beans	fava or lima beans
chicory	endive
cling film	plastic wrap
cornflour	cornstarch
courgettes	zucchini
cream, single	cream, light
cream, double	cream, heavy
flour, plain	flour, all-purpose
frying pan	skillet
grill	broil/broiler
minced meat	ground meat
prawn	shrimp
shortcrust pastry	basic pie dough
spring onion	scallion
sultana	golden raisin
swede	rutabaga

INTRODUCTION

All food can play a role in a healthy diet. Healthy eating means eating a wide variety of foods in the correct proportions, cooked by different methods. It is wrong to think of some foods as being 'healthy' and others as being 'unhealthy'; it is more correct and practical to divide foods into groups according to the proportions in which they should be eaten.

Fat plays an important role in the diet as a source of energy and nutrients – it must not be eliminated but must be limited. Of the total energy intake, no more than 35 per cent should be derived from fat. Saturated fats should not provide more than 10 per cent of the energy intake. The majority of the fat consumed should be based on monounsaturated sources (up to 17 per cent), leaving a recommended maximum of 8 per cent for the polyunsaturated fats. Animal fats and some fats from vegetable sources (notably coconut fat) are saturated. High fat foods – whether of animal or vegetable origin – should not form a large part of the diet. Butter, margarine, cream, full-fat cheeses, oils and fatty meats or products rich in these ingredients should be eaten in moderation or set aside for occasional consumption only.

Sugar, its products and other sweeteners, such as honey, should also be limited in the diet. Eating large amounts of sugar or very sweet foods encourages tooth decay. Eating too many sweet foods may mean that other more nutritious foods are not eaten in sufficient quantities or it can result in problems of overweight or obesity.

On the positive side, fruit, vegetables, starchy foods and foods which provide fibre should make up a large proportion of the diet. The starchy foods should provide the majority of the energy requirements, fibre should be obtained from cereal origins as well as from vegetable sources, and fresh fruit and vegetables are also important as a source of certain vitamins. We should aim to include five different pieces of fruit or vegetables in the diet every day – this includes any portions of fresh fruit, cooked vegetables, salads and significant portions of salad in chunky sandwiches.

Alongside the choice of foods in the diet, the cooking methods used are important. There should be emphasis on regularly eating some raw fruit and vegetables. Avoid frequently cooking by methods which call for adding significant amounts of additional fat – deep frying is the most obvious method which should be set aside for rare use; shallow frying and stir frying should use the minimum of extra fat, and grilling without extra fat is the better option on a day-to-day basis. Overcooking vegetables by boiling them in large amounts of water must be avoided as nutrients are lost to the cooking water. Never add bicarbonate of soda to the cooking water for vegetables as this destroys vitamin C.

Following a healthy eating plan does not mean analysing every meal nor anxiously assessing everything consumed over 24 hours: the correct approach is to consider meals over a few days or a week and in the long term.

The recipes in this book have been selected as much for ease of preparation as for their role in a balanced diet. The emphasis throughout is on including a good range of foods, recipes and cooking methods in the diet, at the same time recognizing practical considerations, such as the cost of food and the use of labour-saving appliances or modern food storage facilities. A guide to food value is included with each recipe, providing information on the protein, carbohydrate, fat, fibre and energy value (kcals). As well as using this information for an occasional check on the content of your diet, you may find it helpful to compare different recipes or to compare the food value of home cooking with some of the information on bought ingredients and cooked products.

NUTRITION AND DIET

A basic understanding of nutrition leads to an awareness of the food we eat in relation to its use by the body and, consequently, to an appreciation of the importance of eating a balanced diet.

Food is the essential fuel for life, maintaining the body as well as building and repairing it. Foods are made up of a combination of different nutrients and, as the body digests the food, these nutrients are released and utilized. General guidelines are provided regarding the nutritional needs of the population; however, individual requirements vary. Factors that influence any one person's dietary needs include gender, age, build, lifestyle and health.

BALANCED DIET

A balanced diet provides all the essential nutrients and sufficient energy to meet an individual's needs and to maintain a healthy body weight without causing obesity. In young people, the diet must also include sufficient nutrients to sustain growth. Nutritional requirements relating to pregnancy, lactation, illness and special conditions should be provided by a doctor and/or dietician.

A balanced diet should include a wide selection of different types of foods, prepared and cooked in a variety of ways. Fresh foods and 'whole' foods are important in providing a balanced variety of nutrients. Raw and lightly cooked fruit and vegetables are also essential.

In general terms, the carbohydrate and vegetable content of the diet should dominate the protein and fat. A diet that lacks carbohydrate, fruit and vegetables is likely to have too high a fat content and to be lacking in fibre. Fibre, from vegetable and cereal sources, is also a vital ingredient for a balanced diet.

BASIC GUIDE TO NUTRIENTS

Protein

Used by the body for growth and repair, protein foods are composed of amino acids, in various amounts and combinations according to the food. There are eight specific amino acids which are an essential part of an adult's diet as they cannot be manufactured by the body from other foods; an additional one is necessary for young children, to sustain their rapid growth. In addition, nine other amino acids are widely available in protein foods, although a high intake of these is not vital as the human body can manufacture them if they are not adequately supplied by the diet.

The quality of any one protein food is determined by the number and proportion of amino acids it contains. Animal foods have a higher biological value than vegetable foods because they provide all the essential amino acids. Generally, no single vegetable food provides all the essential amino acids and they are not present in the proportions best suited to the human body. There are, however, important exceptions to this rule; certain non-animal foods are excellent sources of protein, notably soya beans, some types of nut and mycoprotein (quorn). Other beans and pulses, nuts and cereals are also excellent sources of good-quality protein. Since the amino acid content of vegetable foods varies, by mixing different foods and eating them in sufficient amounts, the necessary types and quantities of amino acids may be obtained.

As amino acids are not stored in a digestible form in the body, a regular supply is essential. This is most easily obtained from a mixture of animal and vegetable sources; if fish, poultry and meat are not eaten, then it is vital that a broad selection of vegetable sources and dairy foods are included to provide sufficient quantities of amino acids.

Carbohydrates

These are the energy-giving foods and may be divided into two main categories: starches and sugars. Starch is obtained from vegetables, cereals, some nuts and under-ripe bananas; sugar is found in fruit (including ripe bananas), honey, molasses and cane sugar.

Carbohydrates in the form of starch, known as complex carbohydrates, should form a significant proportion of the diet. For example, they should be eaten in larger quantities than protein foods, such as meat, poultry and fish. The sugar content of the diet should be limited.

If the diet is deficient in carbohydrates, the body will break down other foods to supply energy, eventually including proteins which have a more valuable role to play.

Fibre

At one time referred to as roughage, fibre is a complex carbohydrate which is not totally digested and absorbed by the body; however, it is vital as a carrier of moisture and waste products through the digestive system.

Fibre is obtained from cereals and vegetables. Good sources are wholegrain rice, oats, wholemeal flour and its products. Sources of vegetable fibre include beans and pulses, some types of fruit, as well as vegetables.

Raw and lightly cooked foods (where appropriate) generally provide more fibre than well-cooked foods; similarly more refined foods offer less fibre than wholefoods and unrefined ingredients.

Fats

Fat and oils provide energy as well as being important sources of certain vitamins and fatty acids. They may be loosely divided into saturated fats and unsaturated fats. Unsaturated fats may be further grouped into polyunsaturated and monounsaturated, depending on their chemical compositions. Although the majority of fatty foods contain both saturated and unsaturated fats, as a general rule animal sources have a higher proportion of saturated fats and vegetable sources are richer in unsaturates.

The recommended fat intake is calculated as a percentage of the total energy value of the diet. The energy value (in calories or joules) of fat eaten should be no more than 35% of the total energy intake with the major proportion of fat in the diet being the unsaturated type.

It is important to remember that young children (under five years of age) should not follow low-fat diets. Although their meals should not contain high proportions of fatty foods (fried foods, chips, high-fat snacks), their fat intake should not be limited by the use of skimmed milk, low-fat cheese and so on.

Vitamins

Although each of the vitamins has specific functions within the body, they also play vital roles in regulating metabolism, helping to repair tissues and assisting in the conversion of carbohydrates and fats into energy. Vitamin deficiency results in general poor health as well as certain specific illnesses.

Vitamins fall into two groups; fat-soluble and water-soluble. Fat-soluble vitamins include A, D, E and K; water-soluble vitamins include C and B-group vitamins. Fat-soluble vitamins can be stored by the body, whereas any excess of the water-soluble type is passed out. This means that a regular supply of water-soluble vitamins is essential and that an excess is unlikely to be harmful. Conversely, the fat-soluble vitamins which are stored in the body should not be consumed to excess as this can result in a condition known as hypervitaminosis. It is important to remember that an excess can be dangerous when taking vitamin supplements, or when eating a very high proportion of foods which are particularly rich in any one (or more) of the fat-soluble vitamins.

Vitamin A Found in fish liver oils, liver, kidney, dairy produce and eggs, vitamin A is important to prevent night blindness. It also contributes to the general health of the eyes and to the condition of the skin. Carotene, found in carrots and yellow or dark green vegetables such as peppers and spinach, can be converted into vitamin A in the body.

If the diet is excessively rich in vitamin A, or supplements are taken for a prolonged period, it is possible for stores to build up to toxic levels in the human liver.

B-group Vitamins This is a large group of water-soluble vitamins, linked because of their importance and use in the body. They play vital roles in promoting chemical reactions, in the release of energy from food and in the efficient functioning of the nervous system. They are essential for general good health and deficiency diseases occur comparatively quickly if these vitamins are missing from the diet.

Thiamin (vitamin B1), riboflavin (vitamin B2), vitamin B12, vitamin B6 (pyridoxine), nicotinic acid, folate, pantothenic acid and biotin are all included in this group (or complex) and each has its own particular characteristics.

In general, meat, offal, dairy produce, and cereals are good sources of B-group vitamins. Some of these vitamins are destroyed by prolonged cooking, notably thiamin, and long exposure to sunlight destroys riboflavin which is found in milk. Refined flour and bread are fortified with thiamin to meet natural levels in comparable wholemeal products. Breakfast cereals are also enriched with, or naturally rich in, B-group vitamins.

Vitamin C or Ascorbic Acid A water-soluble vitamin, this cannot be stored in the body, therefore a regular supply is essential. The main function of this vitamin is to maintain healthy connective tissue (the cell-structure within the body) and healthy blood. It also plays an important role in the healing of wounds. A deficiency can lead to susceptibility to infections.

Vitamin C is found in fresh and frozen vegetables, notably peppers and green vegetables, and in fruit, particularly blackcurrants and citrus fruit. Many fruit juices and drinks are fortified with vitamin C. Potatoes are also a valuable supply; although they are not a rich source, when eaten regularly and in quantity they make an important contribution to a healthy diet.

Vitamin C is the most easily destroyed of all vitamins and may be affected by light, heat, staleness, exposure to air and overcooking. The vitamin is also destroyed by alkaline substances, such as bicarbonate of soda.

NOTE Raw, fresh fruit and vegetables and lightly-cooked vegetables are an important source of vitamins, particularly C. Vegetables should be freshly prepared and cut up as little as possible before cooking. They should not be soaked in water. Cook them lightly and quickly in the minimum of liquid and use the cooking liquid, whenever suitable, in sauces and soups to benefit from any vitamins lost in seepage.

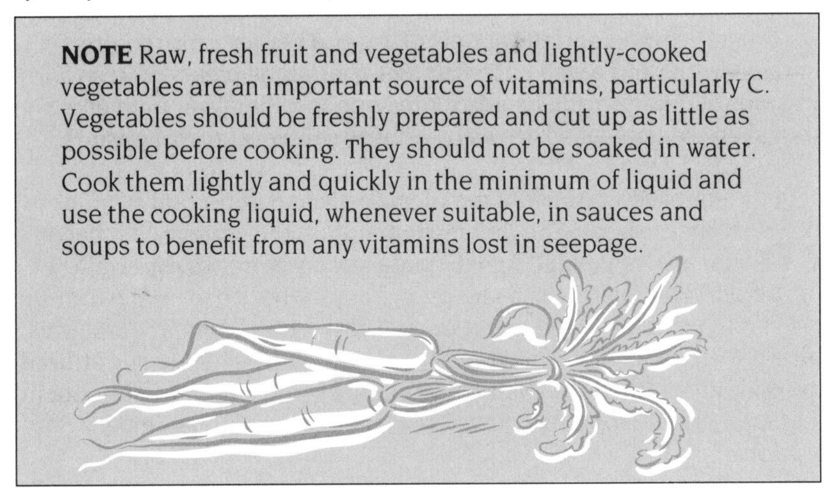

Vitamin D Essential in promoting calcium absorption, a deficiency will result in an inadequate supply of calcium being made available for building and repairing bones and teeth. A diet which is too rich in vitamin D can result in excessive calcium absorption and storage which can be damaging, so supplements should only be taken on medical advice.

Vitamin D is manufactured by the body from the action of sunlight on the skin – this is the primary source for most adults. The vitamin is naturally present in cod liver oil and oily fish such as herrings, mackerel, salmon and sardines. Eggs contain vitamin D, and it can also be manufactured from vegetable sources. Some foods, such as margarine, are fortified with vitamin D.

Vitamin E This vitamin is found in small amounts in most foods and the better sources include vegetable oils, eggs and cereals (especially wheatgerm).

Its role in the body is not clearly established, although unsubstantiated claims are made about its contribution to fertility and its role in improving circulation.

Vitamin K Widely found in vegetables and cereals, this vitamin can be manufactured in the body. Vitamin K contributes towards normal blood clotting. Deficiency is rare, due to a ready supply being available in a mixed diet.

A broad mixed diet, including plenty of raw and lightly cooked fruit and vegetables as well as animal and dairy foods, is likely to provide an adequate supply of vitamins. The value of fresh foods, dairy produce, bread and cereals is obvious. Deficiency can occur in restricted diets where meat and poultry are not eaten and corresponding levels of vitamins are not taken from dairy products or cereals. Those following a vegan diet are most vulnerable, and a diet free of animal products is not recommended.

Minerals

Minerals and trace elements are essential for a healthy body as they play important roles in metabolic processes relating to to the nervous system, glands, muscle control and the supply of water. They are only required in minute quantities and a well balanced diet containing plenty of fresh and whole foods should provide an adequate supply. Mineral supplements should only be taken on medical advice as overdoses can upset metabolism.

Iron An essential constituent of red blood cells and important in muscles, iron can be stored in the body. The diet must maintain the store as, if it becomes depleted, anaemia can result. An adequate supply of iron is especially important during menstruation and pregnancy, as both use up the iron supply.

Found in meat, offal and green vegetables, such as spinach, and eggs, the iron in meat and offal is the most readily absorbed; it is less easily utilized from vegetable sources. The availability of vitamin C is important to promote iron absorption; other factors, such as the presence of tannin, can impair absorption.

Calcium Important in building and maintaining healthy teeth and bones, as well as for normal blood clotting, muscle function and a healthy nervous system, calcium is obtained from milk, cheese, bread, fortified flour and vegetables. The calcium found in milk and dairy produce is likely to be more easily absorbed than that in green vegetables or whole grains (although the system can adjust to utilizing the mineral from less ready sources) and an adequate supply of vitamin D is necessary for efficient calcium absorption.

Phosphorus Along with calcium, this is valuable for bones and teeth. It is widely distributed in food and deficiency is unknown in man.

Potassium, Chlorine and Sodium These play an important role in the balance of body fluids and they are essential for muscle and nerve function. Sodium and chlorine are added to food in the form of salt; sodium is found naturally in meat and milk, and it is added to bread, cereal products and manufactured foods. Potassium is found naturally in meat, vegetables and milk.

Trace Elements These are required by the body in very small amounts and include iodine, fluorine, magnesium, zinc, manganese, cobalt, selenium, molybdenum and chromium. An adequate supply of trace elements is almost always found in the diet and deficiency is extremely rare. Unprescribed supplements should be avoided as they can be detrimental to health.

SPECIFIC NEEDS

Most people have particular dietary needs at some time during their life, if only as babies or young children.

Babies

Breast milk is the ideal food for young babies as it provides all the nutrients they require for the first few months of life. Even if this method of feeding is not continued in the long term, it is a very good idea to breast-feed a baby for the first few days, as valuable antibodies are passed from the mother to help the baby fight infection in the early months.

Bottle-fed babies should be given one of the manufactured milk formulas. These should be prepared exactly according to the manufacturer's instructions or according to the health visitor's or doctor's advice.

Regular checks on the baby's progress are important and any problems should be brought to professional attention immediately.

The weaning process varies from infant to infant; however, between the ages of four to six months a baby should be ready to try a little solid food. By eighteen months, the infant should be able to cope with a mixed diet based on adult foods, following general guidelines for balanced eating. Milk is still an important supplement during this time of rapid growth.

Toddlers and Young Children

Fads and eating difficulties are common in young children, who are too busy discovering the world around them to concentrate for the length of time necessary to learn about meals. Since toddlers and young children are quickly satisfied, it is important that they are introduced to good eating habits and that their meals are nutritious; sweet or fatty snacks are to be avoided and bread, milk, vegetables, fruit, cheese and other valuable foods should be introduced. New foods should be presented in small amounts along with familiar ingredients. Milk is still an important source of nutrients, particularly for difficult eaters.

Providing a meal-time routine and making the process of eating a pleasure is all-important. Children should not be encouraged to play with food, but they should look forward to eating it. Small, frequent yet regular meals, are ideal: in theory, these occasions should be relaxed, free of distractions from the business of eating, and traumatic scenes relating to food rejection should be avoided.

School Children

Fast-growing and active children need a highly nutritious diet, so the substitution of sweets, fatty snacks, sweet drinks and sticky cakes for meals should be avoided. These types of foods should be rare treats.

Breakfasts and packed lunches need special attention. The first meal of the day should be nutritious and provide sufficient energy to keep the child on the move until lunchtime: bread, cereals and milk, eggs and fruit are all practical and useful foods. Raw vegetables, semi-sweet biscuits and crackers are practical mid-morning snack foods but they should not spoil the appetite for lunch. Packed lunches, if eaten, should contain a variety of foods – bread, salad vegetables, some form of protein and a piece of fruit. If a packed lunch is the norm, tea and an early supper are important meals.

As a general guide, every meal should provide growing children with a good balance of valuable nutrients, and additional milk drinks (whole or semi-skimmed) are excellent sources of the calcium which is so important for strong teeth and bones, as well as other nutrients. Sweet foods and confectionery should be avoided as they cause tooth decay and can lead to obesity; similarly, fatty cooking methods and high-fat foods should not be a regular feature in the diet. The importance of fibre, raw fruit and vegetables must be stressed.

Adolescents and Teenagers

This group also requires a highly nutritious, energy-packed diet, but unfortunately, young people are particularly prone to food fads and fashions and it can be difficult to get a teenager to eat a balanced diet. While it is essential to provide all the necessary nutrients, it is important to avoid obesity in this group. Reduced-calorie diets are not recommended, but over-eating must be controlled and the types of food eaten should be carefully monitored.

During this period of rapid growth and development, adopting an active lifestyle and participating in regular exercise is as important as eating well. Young people in this age group should be encouraged to take an interest in nutrition, food and the relationship between a balanced diet, health and fitness.

Parents should try to pass on an understanding of food shopping, meal planning and food preparation, together with an appreciation of the positive benefits of a good diet. This is particularly important for young people who are about to embark on their first experience of living alone and catering for themselves.

Pregnancy and Lactation

A woman should pay special attention to diet during pregnancy as she will need to provide sufficient nutrients and energy for her own needs as well as those of the growing baby. The nutritional requirements continue after birth and during lactation, when the mother is feeding the new baby. The doctor or clinic should provide dietary advice, recommending supplements as necessary.

The mother's responsibility is to ensure that her diet is varied, with emphasis on foods rich in minerals, vitamins and energy. Sweets, chocolates and foods which satisfy without offering nutritional benefit should be avoided in favour of fruit, vegetables, dairy produce, bread and protein foods.

Elderly People

Problems relating to nutrition and the elderly are often linked to social factors. The cost and effort of eating well can deter some elderly people from shopping for a variety of foods and therefore from cooking fresh ingredients. Although many elderly people are extremely active, others may have physical difficulty in shopping or spending long periods standing to prepare meals; in this case help should be sought with planning a practical diet. Equally, dental problems restrict some elderly people from eating well and these can, and should, be overcome by visiting a dentist.

Hot, solid meals are important, particularly in winter. Some elderly people get through the day by eating lots of snacks and this can be detrimental to health; cakes, biscuits and favourite puddings may be pleasant and comforting but they do not constitute a balanced diet. The appetite is often reduced, particularly as the person becomes less active, so meals that are small must contain a high proportion of valuable nutrients. Wholemeal bread, dairy products and cereals with milk are all practical snacks.

The pleasure often disappears from eating when meals are lonely occasions and the palate is not as efficient as it once was. Special centres and meal services exist and these should be used, not only by those who are prevented from cooking for themselves by physical limitations, but also by all who need the company and contact that such services offer.

USING THE FOOD VALUES WITH THE RECIPES

All recipes (except stocks) include a guide to the content of key nutrients: protein, carbohydrate, fat and fibre.

- Where less rich alternatives are given for high-fat foods, the food values are based on the lighter ingredient. For example if an ingredients list includes either cream or fromage frais, the food values reflect the latter.
- Values are based on very low-fat fromage frais where applicable.
- Optional ingredients are not included in food values.
- Total values and values per portion are provided. The values per portion relate to the number of servings suggested at the end of the recipe unless otherwise stated. Where a range of servings is given, the number used in the calculation is given in brackets in the chart.
- Quantities are expressed in grammes (g) and rounded up to the nearest whole figure. Where a value is less than 1g, a dash indicates that the content of that nutrient is negligible in the context of this information.

A GOOD BREAKFAST

THE MOST IMPORTANT MEAL OF THE DAY

Since its heyday in Victorian and Edwardian times, the British breakfast has lapsed into simplicity or even total neglect. The idea of consuming a multi-course cooked breakfast is no longer fashionable, nor is it practical for either domestic or health reasons. However, it is not recommended that this first meal of the day be overlooked. The trend towards missing breakfast completely, then eating sweet or high-fat snacks later in the morning often reflects a poorly balanced diet and a need for change.

Energy-giving Food for Active People

Breakfast should provide energy for the day ahead, particularly in the case of young children, active teenagers and those who perform any type of manual work. Young school children, who still have comparatively small appetites for individual meals, rely on breakfast to see them through the morning. For adults, for whom this meal may not be a main source of nutrients such as protein and vitamins, it provides a good opportunity for topping up the fibre content of the diet.

A Simple Menu

A simple breakfast is usually the healthiest choice – cereals with milk, fresh fruit and bread or rolls are ideal. Allowing children to eat very sweet breakfast cereals encourages them to develop an inappropriate taste for sugary foods and a diet with a high sugar content promotes tooth decay. Lightly sweetened cereals are ideal and porridge makes a satisfying winter breakfast.

Eating a couple of slices of hot toast dripping with butter or margarine every day probably means that the diet includes too much fat. Crisp toast, rolls or thick slices of bread, lightly buttered, are better.

A Variety of Foods

Ideally the breakfast menu should be varied, including cereal or porridge and fruit; yogurt or fromage frais; poached, boiled or scrambled eggs; bread rolls, plain buns, a sandwich or toast. As well as grapefruit, which usually requires some preparation, bananas, apples and pears are satisfying, quick and easy to eat. Grilled bacon with poached eggs or grilled kidneys with tomatoes are also suitable options.

Occasional Traditional Breakfasts

There is absolutely nothing wrong with indulging in the occasional traditional cooked breakfast – bacon, eggs, sausages, mushrooms, tomatoes and fried bread – but eating a comparatively high-fat meal of this type frequently is not advisable.

Muesli

Serve muesli with milk (skimmed, semi-skimmed or whole), yogurt or unsweetened apple juice. Fresh fruit may be added to the cereal – sliced banana and apple when serving with milk, or orange and grapefruit segments to go with yogurt.

FOOD VALUES	TOTAL	PER PORTION (4)
Protein	37g	9g
Carbohydrate	227g	57g
Fat	31g	8g
Fibre	43g	11g
kcals	1283	321

200 g/7 oz mixed grains, such as natural wheat bran, maize meal, wheat meal and oat flakes
30 ml/2 tbsp chopped mixed nuts
30 ml/2 tbsp raisins
30 ml/2 tbsp dried apple flakes
12 dried apricots
30 ml/2 tbsp soft light brown sugar

Mix the grains, mixed nuts, raisins, apple flakes and apricots in a large bowl. Stir in the sugar. Store in a sealed polythene tub or airtight jar until required.

SERVES 4 TO 6

VARIATION

Roasted Muesli The nuts and grains may be dry roasted together in a large, heavy-bottomed frying pan or saucepan. Cook them steadily over low to medium heat, stirring or shaking the pan often, until the nuts and lighter-coloured grains are lightly browned. Allow to cool before mixing with the fruit.

NUTRITION NOTE

Oats are a valuable source of soluble fibre, particularly when eaten raw, as in muesli. The particular type of fibre in oats is believed to make a positive contribution to the way in which the body uses the cholesterol it generates itself.

Traditional Porridge

This is the Scottish way of cooking and serving porridge – made with water and served with cold milk, it provides plenty of energy and valuable fibre but is not a rich source of other nutrients. Both this and the following recipe may be made with milk instead of water or with half milk and half water. Porridge made with milk is richer and more creamy; it is also a more nutritious breakfast dish. Adults may prefer to use semi-skimmed or skimmed milk, depending on the other sources of fat in their diets.

FOOD VALUES	TOTAL	PER PORTION
Protein	11g	3g
Carbohydrate	65g	16g
Fat	8g	2g
Fibre	6g	2g
kcals	355	89

100 *g/4 oz rolled oats*
5 *ml/1 tsp salt*

TO SERVE
demerara sugar
cold milk

Bring 750 ml/1 ¼ pints water to the boil in a saucepan. Sprinkle in the porridge oats, stirring all the time and add the salt. Bring back to the boil, stirring, then reduce the heat so that the porridge simmers. Cover and cook gently for 8-10 minutes, stirring occasionally to prevent the porridge from sticking to the pan.

Ladle the porridge into bowls, leaving plenty of room for the milk to be added, and serve at once. Sprinkle with sugar and pour in cold milk to taste.

SERVES 4

Oatmeal Porridge

FOOD VALUES	TOTAL	PER PORTION
Protein	17g	4g
Carbohydrate	99g	25g
Fat	14g	4g
Fibre	11g	3g
kcals	563	166

150 *g/5 oz coarse or fine oatmeal*
5 *ml/1 tsp salt*

TO SERVE
sugar
cold milk

Bring 1 litre/1¾ pints water to the boil in a heavy-bottomed or non-stick saucepan. Sprinkle in the oatmeal, stirring all the time. Bring just to the boil, stirring, then reduce the heat so that the porridge barely simmers. Cover the pan and cook for 10 minutes.

Stir in the salt and continue cooking for a further 20-30 minutes, until the porridge is thick and smooth. Stir occasionally to prevent the porridge from sticking to the pan. Ladle the porridge into bowls and serve at once. Sprinkle with sugar and pour in cold milk to taste.

SERVES 4

Junket

The temperature is important in the making of junket: if it is too hot or too cold, it will not set. Also it is important to use fresh milk. Homogenized milk gives a very light set but UHT and sterilized milk will not set. This is due to the structure of the milk preventing the rennet culture from working.

FOOD VALUES	TOTAL	PER PORTION
Protein	19g	5g
Carbohydrate	45g	11g
Fat	23g	6g
Fibre	–	–
kcals	455	114

600 ml/1 pint milk
15 ml/1 tbsp sugar
few drops of vanilla essence
5 ml/1 tsp rennet essence
grated nutmeg or ground cinnamon

In a saucepan, warm the milk to blood-heat (about 37°C/98°F) with the sugar and vanilla essence. Stir in the rennet essence.

Pour the mixture into 1 large or 4 small dishes. Cover and leave to stand in a warm place for about 1 hour or until set. Do not move the junket at this stage.

Sprinkle the junket with spice and serve cold but not chilled.

SERVES 4

VARIATION

Almond Junket Instead of the vanilla essence, add 2.5 ml/½ tsp almond essence to the milk. Decorate with toasted almonds, if liked.

Lemon or Orange Junket Infuse the pared rind of 1 lemon or orange in the milk. Do not use any other flavouring.

Eggs for Breakfast

Eggs are nutritious and practical for breakfast but it is important to avoid having the same cooked breakfast every day. Boiled and poached eggs are the better choice for everyday breakfasts, served with lightly buttered crisp toast. Poached eggs may be served with grilled bacon or poached smoked haddock for a traditional breakfast. A full cooked British breakfast should be an occasional treat.

Scrambled eggs are popular for breakfast. Get into the habit of being mean with the butter when scrambling eggs (except for a treat) – cooking them in the microwave is an excellent way of achieving creamy results without the addition of any butter or margarine.

Cooking Eggs

Boiling Bring the eggs to room temperature before cooking to avoid cracking the shells if they are very cold. If an egg does crack, add 15 ml/1 tbsp vinegar or lemon juice to the cooking water to set the white quickly as it escapes.

Bring a small saucepan of water to the boil, allowing enough water to cover the eggs. Place an egg on a spoon and lower it into the water. Begin timing the cooking as soon as the egg is in the water. Regulate the heat so that the water is just boiling. Timing for boiled eggs is very personal but the following provides a guide when cooking average-sized eggs (sizes 3-4):

Soft boiled (soft set white)	3½ minutes
Medium (soft yolk, firm white)	4-4¾ minutes
Hard (firm white, just firm yolk)	10 minutes

Poaching Pour 5 cm/2 inches water into a pan – a frying pan is ideal. Add 15 ml/1 tbsp cider vinegar and bring just to simmering point. Crack a fresh egg on to a saucer. Use a draining spoon to swirl the water in the pan, then slide the egg into the middle of the gentle swirl. (The swirling water gives the egg a good shape.) Simmer for about 3 minutes, or until the egg is set. Spoon the simmering water over the egg to set it evenly. Up to four eggs may be cooked at the same time in a frying pan. Use a slotted spoon to drain the eggs as they are cooked. Trim the edges of the whites and serve at once.

Scrambled Eggs Allow 2 eggs per person. Put the eggs in a bowl. Add 15-30 ml/1-2 tbsp milk for each pair of eggs. Sprinkle in salt and pepper to taste and beat lightly. Melt a little butter in a small saucepan. There should be just enough butter to cover the bottom of the pan; do not allow it to become too hot. Pour in the eggs. Cook gently, stirring or whisking all the time, until the eggs are lightly set and creamy. Remove from the heat and serve at once. If the eggs are allowed to stand in the hot pan or left on the heat, they will set firmly and separate into curds and a thin liquid.

Baking Plain baked eggs should be cooked in individual ovenproof dishes, such as ramekins or the slightly deeper, rounded cocotte dishes. Eggs which are baked with additional ingredients also cook successfully in a large dish; for example, eggs may be baked in hollows among vegetables such as spinach or ratatouille. For the basic method of baking eggs, follow the recipe for Eggs in Cocottes (below).

Eggs in Cocottes

Serve crisp wholemeal toast with baked eggs. Thinly sliced and lightly sautéed mushrooms, a little chopped cooked ham and/or peeled and diced tomatoes may be placed in the bottom of the dishes before adding the eggs.

FOOD VALUES	TOTAL	PER PORTION
Protein	32g	8g
Carbohydrate	3g	1g
Fat	49g	12g
Fibre	–	–
kcals	577	144

25 g/1 oz butter
4 eggs
salt and pepper
60 ml/4 tbsp milk or cream

Butter 4 ramekins or cocottes at least 3.5 cm/1¼ inches deep, and stand them in a baking tin containing enough warm water to come halfway up their sides. Set the oven at 180°C/350°F/gas 4.

Break an egg into each warm dish and add salt and pepper to taste. Top with any remaining butter, cut into flakes. Spoon 15 ml/1 tbsp milk or cream over each egg.

Bake for 6-10 minutes, depending on the thickness of the dishes. The whites of the eggs should be just set. Wipe the outsides of the dishes and serve.

SERVES 4

Home-made Yogurt

Yogurt can easily be made at home. It will not always have the consistency of the commercial product, but the results will be successful if a few simple rules are followed. The yogurt will keep for 4-5 days in a refrigerator. A new carton of commercial yogurt will be needed for the next incubation.

The yogurt can be incubated in one of three ways:

- In an electric, thermostatically-controlled incubator. These are very useful if the family eats a lot of yogurt.
- In a wide-necked vacuum flask (a narrow-necked flask is not suitable as the yogurt is broken up when it is removed). This is suitable for smaller quantities of yogurt.
- In a home-made incubator made from a large biscuit or cake tin with a lid. Line the base and sides with an insulating material such as woollen fabric or cotton wool and have a piece of material large enough to fit inside the top. Use 4 or 5 screw-topped glass jars that will fit inside the incubator.

Method

- Sterilize all the equipment by immersion in boiling water for at least 3 minutes or by using a commercial sterilizing solution.
- Heat 500 ml/17 fl oz UHT or sterilized milk to 43°C/108°F in a saucepan (use a cooking thermometer) and blend in 5 ml/1 tsp fresh natural yogurt. Alternatively, use a yogurt starter culture (obtainable with full instructions from dairy laboratories).
- Pour into pots or glasses, if using. Place in the vacuum flask or prepared incubator, seal, and leave for 6-8 hours.
- Turn the yogurt into a cold bowl and cool rapidly, standing the bowl in cold water and whisking the yogurt until creamy.
- Cover the bowl and chill for about 4 hours when the yogurt will have thickened further.
- When serving, flavour with stewed fruit.

MICROWAVE TIP

Yogurt can be made in the microwave. Heat 600 ml/1 pint milk in a large bowl on High for 6 minutes. Cool until tepid (about 46°C/115°F) and stir in 15 ml/1 tbsp plain yogurt. Add 30 ml/2 tbsp dried full-cream powdered milk. Beat well. Cover the bowl and heat on Low for 70 minutes. Cool, then chill until required.

Using Yogurt

- Plain yogurt may be used in place of cream in savoury and sweet cooking. When heated it may curdle, so stir it into hot sauces, soups and other dishes at the end of cooking. Use plain yogurt in salad dressings, dips and savoury mousses.
- Yogurt combined with flour is less likely to curdle on cooking, for example in quiche fillings or as a topping for savoury bakes.
- Substitute plain yogurt for cream to give a lighter texture and sharper flavour in cold desserts.
- Spread a thick layer of plain yogurt or Greek yogurt over drained canned apricots in a shallow gratin dish. Top with a generous coating of brown sugar and flash under a hot grill to make a special-occasion fruit brûlée.
- Stir clear honey into plain yogurt. Add toasted almonds just before serving.
- Make a tangy fruit jelly by dissolving a jelly tablet in a half quantity of hot water. Allow the jelly to cool before stirring it into an equal quantity of plain yogurt. Pour into a mould or individual dishes. Chill until set.

Yogurt for Breakfast

- Mix diced apple or banana into the yogurt and sprinkle a little muesli on top.
- Spoon yogurt over a simple fresh fruit salad.
- Mix lightly sweetened apple purée into the yogurt.
- Mix roughly chopped, ready-to-eat dried fruit into the yogurt. Apricots, prunes, peaches and apples are all suitable. Sultanas, raisins, dried banana chips and chopped nuts may also be added.
- Mash a banana with yogurt and mix in some bran breakfast cereal.
- Toasted porridge oats and fresh fruit combine well with yogurt.

Stewed Fruit

Stewed fruit may be served hot or cold. A common mistake is to overcook stewed fruit until it is reduced to a pulp. Perfectly stewed fruit should consist of large pieces of tender fruit in a small amount of syrup. The fruit should be washed, dried and prepared according to its type.

Apples	Peel, core and quarter or cut into thick slices.
Blackberries	Pick over, wash and drain.
Blackcurrants	String both redcurrants and blackcurrants.
Gooseberries	Top and tail.
Peaches	Place in a bowl, cover with boiling water and leave for 1 minute, then skin. Halve and remove stones.
Pears	Peel, core and halve, quarter or slice.
Plums	Leave whole or halve and stone.
Rhubarb	Trim and slice into 2.5-5 cm/1-2 inch lengths. If rhubarb is old, peel it thinly to remove any tough strings.

Fruits that discolour should be sprinkled with lemon juice or kept in brine as they are prepared. Drain and thoroughly rinse fruit soaked in brine. Prepare a syrup, allowing 50-175 g/2-6 oz sugar to 150 ml/¼ pint water, depending on the fruit and on personal taste. This quantity is sufficient for 450 g/1 lb fruit. Sharp fruits, such as blackcurrants or rhubarb, may require extra sugar. Dissolve the sugar in the water over low heat, then bring the syrup to the boil. Reduce the heat before adding the fruit, then cover the pan and allow the liquid to simmer very gently so that the fruit yields its syrup to come about one-third of the way up the fruit, although this depends on the size of the pan. Cook the fruit until tender but not mushy, turning large pieces occasionally to cook evenly.

Medium or dry cider (for desserts rather than breakfast), or fruit juice, may be used to make the syrup instead of water. Honey may be added instead of sugar, in which case extra liquid should be used. The cooking syrup may be flavoured with a strip of lemon or orange rind, or with whole spices such as cloves or cinnamon.

Use a large spoon to transfer the fruit to a heatproof serving dish or individual dishes and coat with the cooking syrup. Alternatively, leave the fruit to cool in the covered pan and lightly chill it before serving.

Microwave Stewed Fruit

Most types of fruit cook well in the microwave. Use a large lidded dish or mixing bowl with a plate as a cover. Prepare the syrup first, allowing about 2-3 minutes on High for 150 ml/¼ pint of liquid. The more sugar, the longer the cooking time. Stir the syrup well so that the sugar has dissolved before the fruit is added. Make sure that the fruit is well coated with syrup and cover the dish. Cook the fruit on High, stirring once or twice during cooking. The following is a guide to cooking times for 450 g/1 lb fruit:

apples	4-6 minutes
blackberries	3-5 minutes
blackcurrants	8-10 minutes
gooseberries	5-7 minutes
peaches (4)	4-5 minutes
pears	6-8 minutes
plums	3-5 minutes
rhubarb	6-8 minutes

The exact cooking times depend on the size and ripeness of the fruit. Allow the fruit to stand for 2 minutes before serving or cool and lightly chill.

NUTRITION NOTE

Dried apricots are a good source of iron. Since they are not usually eaten regularly nor in any great quantity, they tend to be overlooked for the iron they can provide. Those following a vegetarian or meat-free diet may find dried apricots a useful source of the mineral in combination with other foods to replace the supply from meat and offal.

Dried Fruit Compote

FOOD VALUES	TOTAL	PER PORTION
Protein	23g	4g
Carbohydrate	211g	35g
Fat	31g	5g
Fibre	25g	4g
kcals	1157	193

100 g/4 oz dried apricots
100 g/4 oz prunes
100 g/4 oz dried figs
50 g/2 oz dried apple rings
30 ml/2 tbsp liquid honey
2.5 cm/1 inch cinnamon stick
2 cloves
pared rind and juice of ½ lemon
50 g/2 oz raisins
50 g/2 oz flaked almonds, toasted

Combine the apricots, prunes and figs in a bowl. Add water to cover and leave to soak. Put the apples in a separate bowl with water to cover and leave both bowls to soak overnight.

Next day, drain both bowls of soaked fruit and make up the liquid to to 600 ml/1 pint with water if necessary. Place the honey in a saucepan with the liquid. Add the cinnamon stick, cloves and lemon rind. Bring to the boil. Stir in the lemon juice.

Add the mixed fruit to the pan, cover and simmer for 10 minutes. Stir in the drained apples and simmer for 10 minutes more, then add the raisins and simmer for 2-3 minutes. Discard the cinnamon, cloves and lemon rind. Spoon the compote into a serving dish and sprinkle with the almonds. Serve warm or cold.

SERVES 6

MICROWAVE TIP

There is no need to pre-soak the dried fruit. Make the honey syrup in a large bowl, using 450 ml/¾ pint water. Microwave on High for about 4 minutes, then stir in all the dried fruit with the cinnamon, cloves and lemon rind. Cover and cook on High for 15-20 minutes or until all the fruit is soft. Stir several times during cooking, each time pressing the fruit down into the syrup.

Orange and Grapefruit Salad

Ortaniques would make a delicious addition to this salad. These juicy citrus fruits are a cross between a tangerine and an orange. Their thin skins make them very easy to peel and segment.

FOOD VALUES	TOTAL	PER PORTION
Protein	9g	2g
Carbohydrate	91g	21g
Fat	1g	–
Fibre	15g	4g
kcals	386	97

4 oranges
2 pink grapefruit
a little caster sugar

Using a vegetable peeler, remove the rind from 1 orange, taking care not to include any of the bitter pith. Cut the rind into strips with a sharp knife. Bring a small saucepan of water to the boil, add the orange strips and cook for 1 minute, then drain and set aside on absorbent kitchen paper.

Peel the remaining oranges and remove all the pith. Using a sharp knife, carefully cut between the segment membranes to remove the flesh. Work over a bowl to catch any juice, and squeeze out all the juice from the remaining pulp. Segment the grapefruit in the same way.

Arrange the citrus segments in concentric circles in a shallow serving dish. Sprinkle the cooked rind over the fruit. Dust with a little sugar and cover, then chill before serving.

SERVES 4

Irish Soda Bread

Soda bread is easy to make and it freezes well, so you can have an occasional batch baking session to provide for many delicious breakfasts in the future. The food values are calculated for white flour and using whole milk. By using wholemeal flour the fibre content can be tripled and the protein value increased by just under a third.

FOOD VALUES	TOTAL	PER PORTION
Protein	65g	5g
Carbohydrate	466g	39g
Fat	20g	2g
Fibre	18g	2g
kcals	2192	183

fat for greasing
575 *g*/1¼ *lb plain or wholemeal flour*
5 *ml*/1 *tsp bicarbonate of soda*
5 *ml*/1 *tsp salt*
5 *ml*/1 *tsp cream of tartar* (*if using fresh milk*)
300 *ml*/½ *pint buttermilk or soured milk or fresh milk*
flour for dusting

Grease a baking sheet. Set the oven at 190°C/375°F/gas 5. Mix all the dry ingredients in a bowl, then make a well in the centre. Add enough milk to make a fairly slack dough, pouring it in almost all at once, not spoonful by spoonful. Mix with a wooden spoon, lightly and quickly.

With floured hands, place the mixture on a lightly floured surface and flatten the dough into a round about 2.5 cm/1 inch thick. Turn on to the prepared baking sheet. Make a large cross in the surface with a floured knife so that the bread heats through evenly.

Bake for about 40 minutes. Pierce the centre with a thin skewer to test for readiness; it should come out clean. Wrap the loaf in a clean tea-towel to keep it soft until required.

MAKES ONE 750 g/1¼ lb LOAF/12 PORTIONS

Mixed Grain Soda Bread Rolls

FOOD VALUES	TOTAL	PER PORTION
Protein	71g	6g
Carbohydrate	379g	32g
Fat	37g	3g
Fibre	33g	3g
kcals	2041	170

fat for greasing
225 *g/8 oz wholemeal flour*
225 *g/8 oz plain flour*
5 *ml/1 tsp bicarbonate of soda*
5 *ml/1 tsp cream of tartar*
5 *ml/1 tsp salt*
60 *ml/4 tbsp rolled oats*
60 *ml/4 tbsp sunflower seeds*
60 *ml/4 tbsp sesame seeds*
60 *ml/4 tbsp cracked wheat*
300 *ml/½ pint milk plus extra for glazing*
flour for kneading

Grease a baking sheet. Set the oven at 200°C/400°F/gas 6. Mix both types of flour in a bowl. Stir in the bicarbonate of soda, cream of tartar, salt, oats, sunflower seeds, sesame seeds and cracked wheat. Mix in the milk to make a soft dough. Turn the dough out on to a lightly floured surface and knead very briefly into a smooth ball.

Divide the dough into 12 equal portions and quickly knead each portion into a round roll. Place the rolls well apart on the baking sheet. Use a sharp knife to cut a cross in the top of each roll. Brush with a little milk, then bake for about 30 minutes, until well risen, golden brown and cooked through. Cool on a wire rack.

MAKES 12

Quick Currant Buns

FOOD VALUES	TOTAL	PER PORTION
Protein	62g	3g
Carbohydrate	486g	20g
Fat	65g	3g
Fibre	16g	1g
kcals	2661	111

fat for greasing
450 *g*/1 *lb plain flour*
2.5 *ml*/½ *tsp cream of tartar*
2.5 *ml*/½ *tsp bicarbonate of soda*
50 *g*/2 *oz butter*
50 *g*/2 *oz caster sugar*
100 *g*/4 *oz currants*
10 *ml*/2 *tsp caraway seeds (optional)*
1 *egg*
300 *ml*/½ *pint milk*
flour for kneading
milk to glaze

Grease a baking sheet. Set the oven at 200°C/400°F/gas 6. Sift the flour, cream of tartar and bicarbonate of soda into a bowl. Rub in the butter, then stir in the sugar, currants and caraway seeds, if used. Make a well in the middle of the dry mixture.

Beat the egg with the milk, pour this into the dry ingredients and mix to form a soft dough. Turn the dough out on to a floured surface and knead it briefly into a smooth ball. Cut the dough into 12 equal portions. Shape each piece of dough into a neat bun and place them slightly apart on the baking sheet.

Brush the buns with a little milk, then bake them for 20 minutes, until risen, well browned and cooked through. Cool on a wire rack. Serve split and buttered.

MAKES 24

MAIN MEALS FOR ALL THE FAMILY

Fish Cakes

Tasty, nutritious, easy to make and popular with children, home-made fish cakes are perfect for midweek family meals.

FOOD VALUES	TOTAL	PER PORTION
Protein	82g	21g
Carbohydrate	74g	19g
Fat	26g	7g
Fibre	5g	1g
kcals	840	210

350 g/12 oz cooked white fish, flaked
450 g/1 lb potatoes
25 g/1 oz butter or margarine
30 ml/2 tbsp milk
15 ml/1 tbsp finely chopped parsley
salt and pepper
50 g/2 oz plain flour
oil for shallow frying

Remove any bones from the fish. Cook the potatoes in a saucepan of boiling water for about 20 minutes, or until tender. Drain thoroughly and mash with a potato masher until smooth. Beat in the butter or margarine and milk. Add the flaked fish and parsley with salt and pepper to taste. Set aside until cold.

Form the fish mixture into 8 portions, shaping each to a flat round cake. Spread out the flour in a shallow bowl, add salt and pepper and use to coat the fish cakes.

Heat a little oil in a frying pan, add the fish cakes and fry for 6-8 minutes, turning once. Drain on absorbent kitchen paper, arrange on a warmed serving dish and serve.

SERVES 4

NOTES ON COOKING METHODS

Buy a good-quality frying pan for shallow frying and use the minimum amount of fat. Alternatively, try using the non-stick sprays which eliminate the need for adding fat to the pan. Fish cakes can be grilled or baked instead of fried. Place them on a greased baking sheet and brush with a little oil, then cook at 200°C/400°F/gas 6 for about 25 minutes. Grill them for 10 minutes on each side.

Fisherman's Hot Pot

FOOD VALUES	TOTAL	PER PORTION
Protein	65g	16g
Carbohydrate	56g	14g
Fat	36g	9g
Fibre	9g	2g
kcals	887	222

2 slices of white bread
30 ml/2 tbsp oil
50 g/2 oz piece of white cabbage, shredded
2 leeks, trimmed, sliced and washed
1 large onion, chopped
225 g/8 oz white fish fillet, skinned and cut into 2.5 cm/1 inch cubes
150 ml/¼ pint dry white wine (optional)
45 ml/3 tbsp tomato purée
1 chicken stock cube
1 bouquet garni
1 garlic clove, crushed
salt and pepper
chopped parsley to garnish

Set the oven at 150°C/300°F/gas 2. Remove the crusts from the bread, cut it into cubes and spread these on a baking sheet. Dry the bread out in the oven for 10-15 minutes, then set aside.

Heat the oil in a large saucepan. Add the vegetables, cover and cook gently for 7-8 minutes until slightly softened. Do not allow the leeks and onion to colour.

Add the fish cubes and fry for 3 minutes, turning occasionally, until firm on all sides. Pour in the wine, if used, and add 1 litre/1¾ pints water. Stir in the tomato purée and crumble in the stock cube. Add the bouquet garni, crushed garlic and salt and pepper to taste.

Heat the stew to simmering point and cook for 20 minutes. Discard the bouquet garni. Pour into a serving dish and sprinkle with the chopped parsley. Serve with the toasted bread cubes.

SERVES 4

NUTRITION NOTE

Fish is a light, protein-rich food which should feature regularly in family meals. Unfortunately, the benefits of eating low-fat fish are often destroyed by coating and deep frying. Grilling, shallow frying in the minimum of fat and stir frying are familiar alternatives, while poaching and casseroling should not be forgotten. Combined with vegetables, white and smoked fish may be used to make delicious sauced dishes.

Fish Pudding

This old-fashioned pudding is light and delicately flavoured, rather similar to fish cakes made with breadcrumbs rather than potato. Remember that a vegetable version of shredded suet is now readily available at major supermarkets; this may be used instead of traditional beef suet if preferred.

FOOD VALUES	TOTAL	PER PORTION
Protein	102g	26g
Carbohydrate	37g	9g
Fat	66g	17g
Fibre	1g	–
kcals	1140	285

fat for greasing
450 *g*/1 *lb white fish fillet (cod, haddock, hake, ling), skinned and finely chopped*
50 *g*/2 *oz shredded suet*
50 *g*/2 *oz fresh breadcrumbs*
30 *ml*/2 *tbsp chopped parsley*
salt and pepper
few drops of anchovy essence
2 *eggs, lightly beaten*
125 *ml*/4 *fl oz milk*
lemon wedges to serve

Grease a 1.1 litre/2 pint pudding basin. Prepare a steamer or half fill a large saucepan with water and bring to the boil.

Combine the fish, suet, breadcrumbs and parsley in a bowl. Mix well and add salt, pepper and anchovy essence. Stir in the eggs and milk. Spoon the mixture into the prepared basin, cover with greased greaseproof paper or foil and secure with string.

Put the pudding in the perforated part of the steamer, or stand it on an old saucer or plate in the saucepan of boiling water. The water should come halfway up the sides of the basin. Cover the pan tightly and steam the pudding for 1-1½ hours.

Leave for 5-10 minutes at room temperature to firm up, then turn out on to a warmed serving plate. Serve with a parsley or mushroom sauce, if liked, or with lemon wedges for their juice.

SERVES 4

Irish Bake

A simple dish that goes down well with the younger members of the family.

FOOD VALUES	TOTAL	PER PORTION
Protein	90g	23g
Carbohydrate	98g	25g
Fat	11g	3g
Fibre	7g	2g
kcals	830	208

butter or margarine for greasing
450 *g*/1 *lb potatoes, thinly sliced*
450 *g*/1 *lb firm white fish fillet, skinned and cut in 2 cm/¾ inch cubes*
1 *small onion, grated*
50 *g*/2 *oz mushrooms, sliced*
salt and pepper
1 (298 *g*/11 *oz*) *can ready-to-serve tomato soup*
chopped parsley to garnish

Grease a shallow ovenproof dish. Set the oven at 200°C/400°F/gas 6. Cook the potatoes in boiling salted water for 10 minutes, then drain well.

Lay the fish in the prepared dish. Top with the grated onion and mushrooms, then add a layer of sliced potatoes. Pour the soup over the potatoes, then bake for 25-30 minutes, or until the fish is cooked and the mixture is bubbling hot. Sprinkle with chopped parsley and serve.

SERVES 4

NUTRITION NOTE

Due to the fact that they are eaten regularly and in some quantity, potatoes are considered to be a valuable source of vitamin C.

Cape Cod Pie

FOOD VALUES	TOTAL	PER PORTION
Protein	121g	30g
Carbohydrate	114g	29g
Fat	83g	21g
Fibre	6g	2g
kcals	1665	416

fat for greasing
450 g/1 lb potatoes, halved
salt and pepper
50 g/2 oz butter or margarine
350 ml/12 fl oz milk plus extra for mashed potatoes
450 g/1 lb cod fillet, skinned
25 g/1 oz plain flour
50 g/2 oz Cheddar cheese, grated
a little cayenne pepper (optional)
1 egg, beaten
pinch of grated nutmeg

Grease an ovenproof dish. Cook the potatoes in boiling water for about 20 minutes or until tender. Drain and mash until smooth. Beat in 25 g/1 oz of the butter or margarine and a little milk to give the potatoes a soft, smooth consistency. Set aside until cold.

Set the oven at 190°C/375°F/gas 5. Place the fish in a saucepan and add the milk. Heat gently until simmering, then continue to cook gently for 5 minutes. Remove and flake the fish, reserving the cooking liquor.

Melt the remaining butter or margarine in a saucepan. Stir in the flour and cook over low heat for 2-3 minutes, without allowing the mixture to colour. Gradually add the reserved milk and cook, stirring constantly until the sauce boils and thickens. Add salt and pepper to taste. Stir in the flaked cod and half the cheese. Add a little cayenne if liked. Remove from the heat.

Set aside about 10 ml/2 tsp of the beaten egg for glazing. Stir the remaining egg into the cold mashed potato. Season with a little nutmeg. Turn the fish mixture into the prepared dish and cover with the potato. Glaze with the reserved egg and bake for 15 minutes, until well browned.

SERVES 4

Cod au Gratin

FOOD VALUES	TOTAL	PER PORTION
Protein	109g	27g
Carbohydrate	89g	22g
Fat	46g	12g
Fibre	16g	4g
kcals	1184	296

fat for greasing
4 (100 g/4 oz) portions of cod fillet
25 g/1 oz butter
2 large onions, finely chopped
100 g/4 oz mushrooms, sliced
salt and pepper
1 green pepper, seeded and diced
450 g/1 lb tomatoes, peeled, seeded and sliced
50 g/2 oz Cheddar cheese, grated
75 g/3 oz fresh white breadcrumbs

Grease a fairly deep ovenproof dish. Set the oven at 190°C/375°F/gas 5. Arrange the cod portions on the base of the dish.

Melt the butter in a frying pan, add the onions and fry gently for 5 minutes until slightly softened. Remove the onions with a slotted spoon and place them on top of the fish. Cook the mushrooms in the same way.

Meanwhile, bring a small saucepan of salted water to the boil, add the diced green pepper and blanch it for 2 minutes. Drain the pepper and add it to the fish, followed by the mushrooms. Top with the tomato slices, salt and pepper.

Combine the cheese and breadcrumbs in a bowl, mix well, then sprinkle over the fish and vegetables. Bake for 30 minutes. Serve at once.

SERVES 4

NUTRITION NOTE

For a low-fat version of the gratin, use the minimum of oil to cook the onion and mushrooms instead of the butter. Continue as in the main recipe but mix 30 ml/2 tbsp grated Parmesan cheese with the breadcrumbs instead of the grated Cheddar.

Haddock in Cider

Pasta and courgettes are suitable accompaniments for this simple fish casserole. For best results, cook sliced courgettes in a covered dish in the microwave – they cook rapidly, retaining all their flavour.

FOOD VALUES	TOTAL	PER PORTION
Protein	109g	25g
Carbohydrate	23g	6g
Fat	14g	4g
Fibre	4g	1g
kcals	684	171

fat for greasing
575 g/1¼ lb haddock fillet, skinned and cubed
225 g/8 oz tomatoes, peeled and sliced
150 g/5 oz mushrooms, sliced
125 ml/4 fl oz dry cider
salt and pepper
30 ml/2 tbsp chopped parsley
25 g/1 oz Cheddar cheese, grated
30 ml/2 tbsp fresh breadcrumbs

Grease a large ovenproof dish. Set the oven at 230°C/450°F/gas 8. Spread out the fish cubes in an even layer on the base of the dish and top with the tomatoes and mushrooms.

Pour the cider over the fish and sprinkle with salt and pepper. Mix the parsley, cheese and breadcrumbs together in a small bowl. Scatter over the fish and bake for 20-25 minutes. Serve at once.

SERVES 4

Smoked Cod and Corn Casserole

FOOD VALUES	TOTAL	PER PORTION
Protein	119g	30g
Carbohydrate	93g	23g
Fat	34g	9g
Fibre	5g	1g
kcals	1127	282

1 (326 *g*/11½ *oz*) *can sweetcorn kernels, drained*
450 *g*/1 *lb smoked cod fillet, skinned and cut in* 1 *cm*/½ *inch strips*
pepper
25 *g*/1 *oz butter or margarine*
125 *ml*/4 *fl oz milk*

Set the oven at 180°C/350°F/gas 4. Drain the corn and spread a layer on the base of an ovenproof dish. Add a layer of cod strips. Season with pepper and dot with butter or margarine.

Repeat the layers until all the corn and cod have been used, then pour over the milk. Cover and bake for 25 minutes. Serve at once.

SERVES 4

VARIATION

Cod and Corn in Sauce Poach the smoked cod fillets, then drain and flake them. Make a white sauce, using 40 g/1½ oz each of butter or margarine and flour, and 600 ml/1 pint milk (or milk mixed with the liquid drained from the can of sweetcorn). Add salt and pepper to taste and stir in the flaked cod and corn. Spoon into an ovenproof dish, top with grated Cheddar cheese and bake for 15-20 minutes at 180°C/350°F/gas 4.

Marinated Mackerel

FOOD VALUES	TOTAL	PER PORTION
Protein	128g	21g
Carbohydrate	–	–
Fat	160g	27g
Fibre	–	–
kcals	1957	326

6 mackerel
parsley sprigs to garnish

MARINADE
100 ml/3½ fl oz olive oil
juice of 1 lemon
fresh thyme sprigs
2 bay leaves
parsley stalks
salt and pepper

Rinse the fish inside and out and pat dry on absorbent kitchen paper. Make 3 diagonal slashes in the flesh on both sides of each fish.

Mix all the ingredients for the marinade in a shallow dish large enough to hold all the fish in a single layer. Add the mackerel, turning to coat them evenly in the marinade. Cover the dish and marinate the fish for 1 hour.

Drain the fish, reserving the marinade, and place on a rack over a grill pan. Grill under moderate heat for 5-7 minutes each side, turning once and basting frequently with the reserved marinade. Serve very hot, garnished with parsley sprigs.

SERVES 6

Roast Chicken with Honey and Almonds

FOOD VALUES	PER PORTION*
Protein	41g
Carbohydrate	8g
Fat	38g
Fibre	–
kcals	537

1 (1.4-1.8 kg/3-4 lb) oven-ready roasting chicken
½ lemon
salt and pepper
45 ml/3 tbsp honey
50 g/2 oz flaked almonds
pinch of powdered saffron
30 ml/2 tbsp oil
watercress sprigs to garnish (optional)

Set the oven at 180°C/350°F/gas 4. Rub the chicken all over with the cut lemon, then sprinkle with salt and pepper. Line a roasting tin with a piece of foil large enough to enclose the bird completely.

Put the bird into the foil-lined tin, then brush it all over with the honey. Sprinkle the nuts and saffron over, then trickle the oil very gently over the top. Bring up the foil carefully, tenting it over the bird so that it is completely covered. Make sure that the foil does not touch the skin. Seal the package by folding the edges of the foil over.

Roast for 1½-2 hours or until the chicken is cooked through. Open the foil for the last 10 minutes to allow the breast of the bird to brown. Transfer the chicken to a heated serving dish and garnish it with watercress if liked.

SERVES 4 TO 6

NUTRITION NOTE

*The food values are based on a 175 g/6 oz portion of chicken with skin.

Spiced Drumsticks

FOOD VALUES	TOTAL	PER PORTION
Protein	83g	21g
Carbohydrate	35g	9g
Fat	45g	11g
Fibre	3g	1g
kcals	872	218

15 *ml/1 tbsp oil*
1 *onion, grated*
1 *garlic clove, crushed*
5 *ml/1 tsp curry powder*
salt and pepper
60 *ml/4 tbsp mango chutney*
8 *chicken drumsticks*

Heat the oil in a small saucepan, then add the onion and garlic. Cook, stirring, for 5 minutes. Add the curry powder and salt and pepper; stir for another minute or so. Remove from the heat. Chop any large pieces of fruit in the mango chutney, add it to the onion mixture and stir well. Set the oven at 200°C/400°F/gas 6.

Make two or three slashes into the skin and flesh on both sides of the drumsticks, then place them in an ovenproof dish. Spoon the onion mixture over and cover with foil. Bake for 30 minutes.

Turn the drumsticks over and baste them with the cooking juices, then continue to cook, uncovered, for a further 20-30 minutes, turning once more, until cooked through and well browned. Serve at once. To serve cold, transfer to a cold dish, cover and cool quickly, then chill until required.

SERVES 4

Barbecued Chicken Drumsticks

FOOD VALUES	TOTAL	PER PORTION
Protein	106g	27g
Carbohydrate	5g	1g
Fat	82g	21g
Fibre	1g	–
kcals	1185	296

25 g/1 oz butter
30 ml/2 tbsp oil
12 chicken drumsticks
60 ml/4 tbsp vinegar
15 ml/1 tbsp Worcestershire sauce
15 ml/1 tbsp tomato purée
5 ml/1 tsp soy sauce
5 ml/1 tsp grated onion
5 ml/1 tsp paprika
2.5 ml/½ tsp salt

Melt the butter with the oil in a small saucepan. Brush a little of the mixture over the chicken drumsticks to coat them thoroughly, then arrange on a rack in a grill pan.

Stir the remaining ingredients into the leftover butter and oil in the pan. Simmer for 2 minutes, then brush a little of the mixture over the chicken. Grill or barbecue over medium coals, turning occasionally and brushing with more sauce until cooked through. Serve with rice or salad.

SERVES 4

HEALTHY ACCOMPANIMENTS

The main meal of the day should be satisfying and nutritious, providing a good portion of protein, including either fish, poultry, meat, offal, dairy produce, pulses or nuts. However the bulk of the meal should be made up of vegetables and/or starchy foods, such as rice or pasta, usually served as accompaniments. It is recommended that the daily diet should include five portions of fruit or vegetables – that is over all meals and snacks eaten.

COOKING METHODS

It is equally important to consider the different cooking methods used when preparing meals throughout the week. There is nothing wrong with frying some foods but deep frying, in particular, should be a seldom-used method. Boiling, poaching, stewing, steaming, grilling, stir-frying or shallow frying in the minimum of fat are all methods to use regularly. On a daily basis, the emphasis should be on cooking foods with little or no additional fat.

CONSERVING NUTRIENTS IN VEGETABLES

- Buy the freshest possible vegetables in quantities you can use quickly.
- Prepare the vegetables shortly before cooking – do not allow them to stand or soak for any length of time.
- Use a stainless steel knife or peeler, or tear green vegetables.
- Remember that the peel on some vegetables, such as potatoes, contains valuable nutrients, so try scrubbing rather than peeling them when possible.
- When boiling, use the minimum water necessary and cook the vegetables for the shortest possible time.
- Use the cooking liquid from vegetables for making sauces or gravy whenever possible.
- Serve the vegetables promptly after cooking.
- Many commercially frozen vegetables are an excellent source of nutrients.

COOKING AND SERVING SUGGESTIONS

Here are a few ideas for serving vegetables, instead of tossing them in butter.

- Add low-fat fromage frais in place of milk and most of the butter when mashing potatoes. Add a little grated nutmeg or plenty of freshly ground white pepper for an excellent flavour.
- Toss boiled potatoes (old or new) with snipped chives, chopped spring onion, mint or parsley and some fromage frais or Greek yogurt instead of adding a large amount of butter.

- Cook a little finely chopped onion or chopped spring onion in 30 ml/ 2 tbsp olive oil until softened or until the spring onion has just wilted. Toss with new or old boiled potatoes instead of seasoning. Add a little grated lemon rind if you like. Onion cooked in olive oil also goes well with green vegetables, such as spinach, cabbage, French or runner beans.
- Both fromage frais and plain yogurt go well with spinach or cabbage.
- Brown flaked or slivered almonds in a little olive or sunflower oil. Toss the nuts into Brussels sprouts, potatoes, peas or carrots.
- Briefly stir fry vegetable mixtures in the minimum of oil. For example, mix onion, carrot and red cabbage; mange tout, spring onions and sweetcorn; onion, spinach and raisins; or halved Brussels sprouts, onion and diced eating apple.
- Steam individual foil packets of mixed vegetables. French beans, carrots, mange tout, button onions, courgettes or leeks are all suitable.

THE VALUE OF SALADS

With year-round availability of high-quality salad ingredients it is a good idea to include as many dishes of raw vegetables as possible in the diet. As well as the usual salad vegetables, such as lettuce, cucumber, tomatoes, spring onions and celery, include cabbage, spinach, green or red peppers, carrots, celeriac, mange tout and courgettes. Fresh raw vegetables are an excellent source of vitamins and they also contribute to the fibre content of the diet.

Serve a side salad in addition to one or two cooked vegetable accompaniments as this will increase the overall balance of vegetables in the diet. Side salads complement rice and pasta dishes, grilled foods, boiled ham and braised or stewed dishes but they do not go with traditional roasts.

HEARTY ACCOMPANIMENTS

Rice, pasta, beans, pulses, grains and cereals all make delicious side dishes for a wide variety of foods.

Considerable emphasis has been placed on the value of whole grains, such as brown rice, which provide valuable fibre; however, it is more interesting to include a variety of different types of rice and to ensure that fibre is obtained by including several alternative foods in the diet, such as breakfast cereals and bread. Whole and cracked wheat, couscous and barley may all be cooked and served instead of rice.

Beans and pulses are satisfying and provide protein as well as fibre. Dried varieties often require soaking before fairly lengthy cooking but canned types are ready for instant use in salads, sauces and stews as well as vegetable dishes. Cooked beans and pulses freeze well, so it is worth boiling them in quantity. They also cook well and quickly in a pressure cooker.

Turkey and Chipolata Hot Pot

This is an excellent way of using up leftovers from a roast turkey. Cooked chicken may be used instead of turkey and the chipolatas will extend a small amount of meat to serve four.

FOOD VALUES	TOTAL	PER PORTION
Protein	148g	37g
Carbohydrate	110g	28g
Fat	83g	21g
Fibre	24g	6g
kcals	1824	456

15 *ml*/1 *tbsp oil*
225 *g*/8 *oz chipolata sausages or cocktail sausages*
1 *onion, halved and sliced*
2 *carrots, diced*
2 *parsnips, diced*
1 *bay leaf*
5 *ml*/1 *tsp dried sage*
45 *ml*/3 *tbsp plain flour*
300 *ml*/½ *pint medium cider*
300 *ml*/½ *pint turkey or chicken stock*
350 *g*/12 *oz cooked turkey, diced*
salt and pepper
100 *g*/4 *oz frozen peas*

Heat the oil in a large flameproof casserole until it runs easily over the base. Add the sausages and turn them in the oil. Sprinkle the onion into the pan and cook, turning occasionally, until the sausages are evenly and lightly browned but not necessarily cooked through. Pour off excess fat from the pan, if necessary.

Add the carrots, parsnips, bay leaf and sage to the casserole. Cover and cook gently for 15 minutes. Stir in the flour, then gradually stir in the cider and stock and bring to the boil. Add the turkey, with salt and pepper to taste, then cover and simmer for 10 minutes, or until the vegetables are tender.

Stir in the peas, replace the cover and simmer for a further 10-15 minutes. Taste and adjust the seasoning before serving. If using chipolatas, cut them into bite-sized chunks before serving.

SERVES 4

Beef and Potato Pie

This is simple country cooking with no frills. Salt and pepper are the only condiments used; the pie deriving its flavour from long slow cooking of meat and vegetables. It is therefore important that the stewing steak is of good quality. Remember that stewing steak gives a better flavour than braising steak in a recipe of this type.

FOOD VALUES	TOTAL	PER PORTION
Protein	158g	26g
Carbohydrate	199g	33g
Fat	74g	12g
Fibre	21g	4g
kcals	2043	341

675 g/1½ lb stewing steak, trimmed and cut into 2 cm/¾ inch cubes
3 onions, sliced
3 large carrots, sliced
1 kg/2¼ lb potatoes, sliced
salt and pepper
hot beef stock (see method)

Set the oven at 160°C/325°F/gas 3. Layer the meat with the onion, carrot and potato slices in an ovenproof casserole, finishing with a neat layer of potatoes. Add salt and pepper.

Pour in enough hot stock to three-quarters cover the contents of the casserole, reserving some stock for adding if the dish begins to dry out during cooking. Cover with a tight-fitting lid or foil and bake for 3-3½ hours, or until the beef is very tender.

About 30-40 minutes before the end of the cooking time, remove the casserole lid to allow the top layer of potato to brown. Serve straight from the casserole.

SERVES 6

MRS BEETON'S TIP

If liked, the top layer of potato may be sprinked with paprika before browning. Use a sweet Hungarian rose paprika if possible.

Meatloaf

Serve boiled new potatoes or baked potatoes and a couple of different vegetables or a salad with this meatloaf.

FOOD VALUES	TOTAL	PER PORTION
Protein	98g	25g
Carbohydrate	33g	8g
Fat	81g	20g
Fibre	2g	1g
kcals	1236	309

oil for greasing
450 g/1 lb minced beef or pork, or a mixture of both
50 g/2 oz fresh breadcrumbs
1 large onion, finely chopped
30 ml/2 tbsp chopped parsley
5 ml/1 tsp chopped fresh thyme
5 ml/1 tsp chopped fresh sage
1 egg
15 ml/1 tbsp Worcestershire *sauce*
salt and pepper

Grease a 450 g/1 lb loaf tin. Set the oven at 180°C/350°F/gas 4. Place all the ingredients in a bowl, adding plenty of salt and pepper. Pound the ingredients with the back of a mixing spoon until thoroughly combined and well bound together.

Turn the mixture into the tin, press it down well and cover the top with a piece of greased greaseproof paper. Bake for 1 hour, until the loaf is firm and has shrunk away from the tin slightly. Turn out and serve hot or cold.

SERVES 4

NUTRITION NOTE

It is best to buy lean minced meat rather than cheaper, fatty mince. Pale minced beef usually has a higher fat content than darker types. The fat content of minced lamb and pork often varies – one of the best ways of obtaining the leanest minced meat is to buy a joint and ask the butcher to mince the meat.

Hamburgers

If you intend serving the burgers less than well cooked, buy good-quality steak and mince it at home. Bought minced steak should be cooked through before serving.

FOOD VALUES	TOTAL	PER PORTION
Protein	109g	27g
Carbohydrate	–	–
Fat	48g	12g
Fibre	–	–
kcals	872	218

450 g/1 lb minced steak
2.5 ml/½ tsp salt
2.5 ml/½ tsp freshly ground black pepper
5-10 ml/1-2 tsp grated onion (optional)

Combine the meat, salt and pepper in a bowl. Add the onion, if used, and mix well. Shape the mixture lightly into four flat round cakes, about 2 cm/¾ inch thick.

Cook the hamburgers under a preheated grill or over coals on a barbecue grill for 6-8 minutes, turning once. Serve plain or in buns, with toppings or fillings as desired.

SERVES 4

VARIATIONS

Offer any or all of the following with the burgers: lettuce leaves; sliced cucumber; sliced tomatoes; sliced gherkins; sliced raw or fried onions; hamburger relish; German or French mustard; tomato ketchup.

Lamb Burgers Use good-quality, lean minced lamb instead of steak. Add 2.5ml/½ tsp dried oregano to the mixture.

Pitta Burgers Make 8 burgers instead of 4 and serve them in warm pitta bread pockets, with shredded lettuce, chopped cucumber and chopped tomatoes. Add a dollop of Greek yogurt, if liked.

Bacon and Apple Patties

This is a good recipe for inexpensive bacon offcuts or for turning a comparatively small amount of bacon into an interesting meal. Serve the patties with baked potatoes, carrots or mashed parsnips and cabbage or a salad.

FOOD VALUES	TOTAL	PER PORTION
Protein	48g	6g
Carbohydrate	76g	10g
Fat	100g	13g
Fibre	5g	1g
kcals	1377	172

225 g/8 oz rindless bacon rashers, chopped (*see* Mrs Beeton's Tip)
1 onion, finely chopped
75 g/3 oz fresh breadcrumbs
salt and pepper
5 ml/1 tsp chopped fresh thyme or 2.5 ml/½ tsp dried thyme
15 ml/1 tbsp chopped fresh sage or 5 ml/1 tsp dried sage
1 cooking apple, peeled, cored and grated
15 ml/1 tbsp sugar
1 egg

In a bowl, mix the bacon, onion, breadcrumbs, a little salt and plenty of pepper, the thyme, sage, apple and sugar. When the ingredients are well combined, mix in enough of the egg to bind the mixture.

Wet your hands and shape the mixture into 8 small round patties. Cook the patties under a grill preheated to moderate for about 10 minutes on each side, until thoroughly cooked through and well browned. Serve freshly cooked.

MAKES 8

MRS BEETON'S TIP

An easy way of cutting bacon rashers into small pieces is by using kitchen scissors. Cut 2 or 3 rashers at a time, first into narrow strips, then across into small pieces.

Pork and Apple Hot Pot

FOOD VALUES	TOTAL	PER PORTION
Protein	88g	22g
Carbohydrate	100g	25g
Fat	168g	42g
Fibre	11g	3g
kcals	2238	560

fat for greasing
1 *cooking apple*
45 *ml*/3 *tbsp oil*
1 *onion, thinly sliced*
100 *g*/4 *oz mushrooms, thinly sliced*
4 *pork loin chops, trimmed*
2.5 *ml*/½ *tsp dried sage or savory*
450 *g*/1 *lb potatoes, cut into* 2 *cm*/¾ *inch cubes*
salt and pepper

GARNISH (OPTIONAL)
12 *slices of eating apple, cored and halved*
parsley sprigs

Set the oven at 180°C/350°F/gas 4. Peel, core and slice the apple. Heat the oil in a large frying pan, add the apple and onion and fry over moderate heat until golden brown.

Put the mushrooms on the base of a large shallow greased casserole. Add the chops and cover with the apple and onion. Sprinkle the herbs over the top. Cover with the potatoes, brushing them with the fat remaining in the pan. Sprinkle with salt and pepper to taste. Pour in enough water to come halfway up the meat and vegetables.

Cover the casserole with foil or a tight-fitting lid. Bake for 1½ hours, removing the covering 30 minutes before the end of the cooking time to allow the potatoes to brown. Garnish with apple and parsley (if used), then serve from the casserole.

SERVES 4

China Chilo

FOOD VALUES	TOTAL	PER PORTION
Protein	105g	26g
Carbohydrate	67g	17g
Fat	134g	34g
Fibre	25g	6g
kcals	1879	470

450 g/1 lb minced lamb
2 onions, finely chopped
1 Iceberg lettuce, shredded
5 ml/1 tsp salt
2.5 ml/½ tsp freshly ground black pepper
150 ml/¼ pint stock (lamb, vegetable or chicken)
450 g/1 lb fresh peas, shelled or 225 g/8 oz frozen peas
30-45 ml/2-3 tbsp chopped fresh mint, tarragon or parsley

Heat the minced lamb in a heavy-bottomed saucepan until the fat runs. Remove the pan from the heat and drain off the fat. Add the onions, then continue to cook, stirring constantly, until the meat is well browned.

Stir in the lettuce with the salt and pepper. Cook, turning the mixture, for 2-3 minutes, then pour in the stock. Bring to the boil, lower the heat, cover the pan with a tight-fitting lid and simmer very gently for 30 minutes. Add the peas and stir well, then replace the lid and cook for a further 30 minutes. Check the pan from time to time and add more stock or water if the mixture is too dry.

Stir in the chopped mint, tarragon or parsley and serve the china chilo hot. Baked or boiled potatoes (particularly new potatoes) are simple accompaniments; alternatively, cooked rice or pasta makes a practical base on which to serve the meat mixture.

SERVES 4

NUTRITION NOTE

When cooking any fatty meats by frying, make a point of pouring away the excess fat from the pan, as emphasized in this recipe. When casseroling or stewing food which yields fat, or when making soup or stock, skim the surface of the liquid before serving to remove the excess fat. Animal fats rise to the surface of liquids on cooling to solidify on chilling and are then easily removed from the surface of cooked dishes.

Irish Stew

Old favourites, like this recipe, have a well-earned place on the dinner table. Since modern rearing methods result in animals that yield leaner meat, dishes made from the less expensive cuts do not have to be fatty but they are well flavoured and economical. Serve two or three vegetables with the stew to make a delicious, well-balanced meal.

FOOD VALUES	TOTAL	PER PORTION (6)
Protein	162g	27g
Carbohydrate	188g	31g
Fat	82g	14g
Fibre	16g	3g
kcals	2084	347

1 kg/2¼ lb middle neck or scrag end of neck of lamb
2 large onions, thinly sliced
1 kg/2¼ lb potatoes, thinly sliced
salt and pepper
well-flavoured lamb or chicken stock
30 ml/2 tbsp chopped parsley to garnish

Set the oven at 190°C/375°F/gas 5. Cut the meat into neat cutlets or pieces, trimming off any excess fat. Layer the meat, onions, and potatoes in a casserole, sprinkling each layer with salt and pepper, and ending with potatoes.

Add enough stock to half fill the casserole. Cover with a lid and bake for about 2-2½ hours, removing the lid for the last 30 minutes of the cooking time, to allow the potato topping to brown. Sprinkle with chopped parsley to serve.

SERVES 4 TO 6

Faggots

FOOD VALUES	TOTAL	PER PORTION (6)
Protein	189g	47g
Carbohydrate	84g	21g
Fat	84g	21g
Fibre	5g	1g
kcals	1820	455

fat for greasing
800 *g*/1¾ *lb pig's liver*
2 *onions, quartered*
2.5 *ml*/½ *tsp dried thyme*
10 *ml*/2 *tsp dried sage*
generous pinch of grated nutmeg
2.5 *ml*/½ *tsp ground mace*
salt and pepper
1 *egg, lightly beaten*
100 *g*/4 *oz fresh white breadcrumbs*
caul fat, pork dripping, lard or butter

Remove the skin and any tubes from the liver and slice it thinly. Put it in a saucepan with the onions. Add just enough water to cover. Bring to the boil, lower the heat, cover and simmer for 30 minutes. Drain. Mince the liver and onions finely or process in a food processor. Add the herbs, spices, seasoning, egg and enough breadcrumbs to make a firm mixture.

Divide the mixture into 8 equal portions and shape into balls. Wrap in caul fat, if used. Lay the faggots side by side in a greased baking tin and dot with fat if caul is not used. Cover the tin loosely with foil. Bake for 25 minutes, then remove the foil and bake for a further 10-15 minutes to brown the tops of the faggots. Serve hot, with a thickened gravy.

SERVES 4 TO 6

MRS BEETON'S TIP

Caul fat is a tough membrane laced with fat. Salted caul is seldom available; however should it be obtained, it must be soaked in cold water for 30 minutes, then thoroughly rinsed and soaked in fresh water with a little vinegar added. Finally, it should be rinsed and spread out on a perfectly clean tea-towel ready for use.

Liver Hot Pot

FOOD VALUES	TOTAL	PER PORTION
Protein	150g	25g
Carbohydrate	159g	26g
Fat	122g	20g
Fibre	12g	2g
kcals	2293	382

fat for greasing
450 *g*/1 *lb lamb's liver, sliced*
45 *ml*/3 *tbsp plain flour*
salt and pepper
2 *large onions, thinly sliced*
800 *g*/1¾ *lb potatoes, thinly sliced*
500 *ml*/18 *fl oz beef stock*
6-8 *rindless bacon rashers*

Set the oven at 180°C/350°F/gas 4. Remove the skin and any tubes from the liver. Mix the flour with salt and pepper in a shallow bowl. Coat the liver slices in the seasoned flour. Shake off excess flour.

Arrange layers of liver, onion and potatoes in a greased casserole, ending with a layer of potatoes. Heat the stock in a small saucepan and pour in just enough to cover the potatoes. Cover the casserole with a lid or foil and bake for 1 hour or until the liver is tender.

Remove the lid and arrange the bacon rashers on top of the potatoes. Return the casserole to the oven for about 15 minutes or until the bacon is browned. Serve immediately, straight from the casserole.

SERVES 6

NUTRITION NOTE

Liver and other offal is lean and nutritious, providing a valuable supply of readily absorbed iron as well as other nutrients. Liver and bacon is a classic combination – select lean bacon to avoid increasing the fat content of a dish.

Kidneys Turbigo

FOOD VALUES	TOTAL	PER PORTION
Protein	104g	26g
Carbohydrate	42g	11g
Fat	100g	25g
Fibre	4g	1g
kcals	1569	392

15 ml/1 tbsp oil
225 g/8 oz cocktail sausages
1 small onion, finely chopped
450 g/1 lb lambs' kidneys, halved and cored
salt and pepper
100 g/4 oz small button mushrooms
15 ml/1 tbsp plain flour
30 ml/2 tbsp tomato purée
150 ml/¼ pint dry white wine
150 ml/¼ pint Vegetable Stock (page 65) or Chicken Stock (page 64)
45 ml/3 tbsp chopped parsley

Heat the oil in a large frying pan, add the sausages and cook them over moderate heat until evenly golden. Using a slotted spoon, transfer them to a dish and set aside. Pour off any excess fat from the pan, leaving enough to cook the remaining ingredients. Add the onion and cook, stirring, for 10 minutes, until softened. Add the kidneys, with salt and pepper to taste. Cook them, turning often, until browned all over and just cooked.

Add the mushrooms to the pan and continue cooking for about 5 minutes, so that the mushrooms are lightly cooked. Use a slotted spoon to transfer the kidneys and mushrooms to the dish with the sausages.

Stir the flour into the fat remaining in the pan. Stir in the tomato purée, then gradually stir in the wine and stock. Bring to the boil, stirring all the time, then lower the heat and return the sausages, mushrooms and kidneys to the pan. Simmer gently for 5 minutes.

Add the parsley and seasoning to taste before serving with cooked pasta or rice.

SERVES 4

Baked Stuffed Marrow

FOOD VALUES	TOTAL	PER PORTION (6)
Protein	100g	17g
Carbohydrate	84g	14g
Fat	136g	23g
Fibre	8g	1g
kcals	1935	323

fat for greasing
1 *marrow*
1 *small onion, finely chopped or grated*
225 *g*/8 *oz minced beef*
100 *g*/4 *oz pork sausagemeat or* 100 *g*/4 *oz extra minced beef*
25 *g*/1 *oz fresh breadcrumbs*
15 *ml*/1 *tbsp chopped parsley*
15 *ml*/1 *tbsp snipped chives*
5 *ml*/1 *tsp* Worcestershire *sauce*
salt and pepper
1 *egg, beaten*

SAUCE
25 *g*/1 *oz butter*
25 *g*/1 *oz plain flour*
300 *ml*/½ *pint milk, stock or mixture (see method)*
75-100 *g*/3-4 *oz* Cheddar *cheese, grated*
pinch of dry mustard

Generously grease a large, shallow casserole. Set the oven at 180°C/350°F/gas 4. Halve the marrow lengthways and scoop out the seeds. Lay the halves side by side in the prepared casserole.

Put the onion into a bowl with the beef, sausagemeat, if used, breadcrumbs, parsley, chives, Worcestershire sauce and salt and pepper. Mix well. Bind the mixture with beaten egg. Avoid making it too moist. Divide the stuffing between each marrow half. Cover the casserole and bake for 1 hour.

Strain off and reserve most of the liquid in the casserole. Meanwhile make the sauce. Melt the butter in a saucepan. Stir in the flour and cook over low heat for 2-3 minutes, without colouring. Over very low heat, gradually add the liquid (the casserole juices may be used), stirring constantly. Bring to the boil, stirring, then lower the heat and simmer for 1-2 minutes until smooth and thickened. Add the cheese, mustard and salt and pepper to taste. Pour the cheese sauce over the marrow and bake, uncovered, for a further 20 minutes, until the sauce topping is golden brown.

SERVES 4 TO 6

Chick-Pea Casserole

A few fresh herb sprigs used as a garnish improve the appearance of individual portions.

FOOD VALUES	TOTAL	PER PORTION
Protein	74g	19g
Carbohydrate	179g	45g
Fat	48g	12g
Fibre	43g	11g
kcals	1402	351

300 *g/11 oz chick-peas, soaked overnight in cold water to cover*
30 *ml/2 tbsp olive oil*
1 *onion, chopped*
1 *garlic clove, crushed*
1 *bay leaf*
1 *green pepper, seeded and sliced*
200 *g/7 oz white cabbage, shredded*
100 *g/4 oz mushrooms, sliced*
1 (397 *g/14 oz) can chopped tomatoes*
2.5 *ml/½ tsp ground ginger*
pinch of ground cloves
salt and pepper
30 *ml/2 tbsp chopped fresh mint*
60 *ml/4 tbsp chopped parsley*

Drain the chick-peas, put them in a saucepan and add fresh water to cover. Do not add salt. Bring to the boil, cook for 10 minutes, then lower the heat and simmer for 1 hour or until tender. Drain the chick-peas, reserving the cooking liquor.

Heat the olive oil in a large saucepan, add the onion, garlic, bay leaf, green pepper and cabbage and fry over moderate heat for 10 minutes. Add the mushrooms, chick-peas and tomatoes. Stir in 125 ml/4 fl oz of the reserved cooking liquor, with the ginger and ground cloves. Add salt and pepper to taste. Bring to the boil, lower the heat and cook very gently for 1 hour, adding more liquid, if required, during cooking. The cooked casserole should be moist, but there should not be too much liquid. Before serving, stir in the mint, parsley and more seasoning if necessary.

SERVES 4

Winter Vegetable Casserole

This simple casserole may be simmered very slowly on the hob, if preferred.

FOOD VALUES	TOTAL	PER PORTION
Protein	19g	5g
Carbohydrate	141g	35g
Fat	73g	18g
Fibre	21g	5g
kcals	1264	316

50 g/2 oz butter
30 ml/2 tbsp oil
2 onions, sliced
1 garlic clove, crushed
2 leeks, trimmed, sliced
225 g/8 oz swede, cubed
100 g/4 oz turnip, cubed
3 carrots, sliced
100 g/4 oz mushrooms, sliced
100 g/4 oz pearl barley, washed
5 ml/1 tsp dried thyme
1 bay leaf
salt and pepper
450 ml/¾ pint Vegetable Stock (page 65)
30 ml/2 tbsp chopped parsley to garnish

Set the oven at 180°C/350°F/gas 4. Melt the butter in the oil in a large flameproof casserole. Add the onions, garlic, leeks, swede, turnip and carrots and fry for about 10 minutes, stirring frequently.

Stir in the mushrooms, barley, thyme and bay leaf, with plenty of salt and pepper. Pour in the stock. Cover the casserole and transfer it to the oven. Bake for 1-1½ hours until all the vegetables are cooked and the barley is tender. Fluff up the grains with a fork, sprinkle the parsley over the top and serve.

SERVES 4

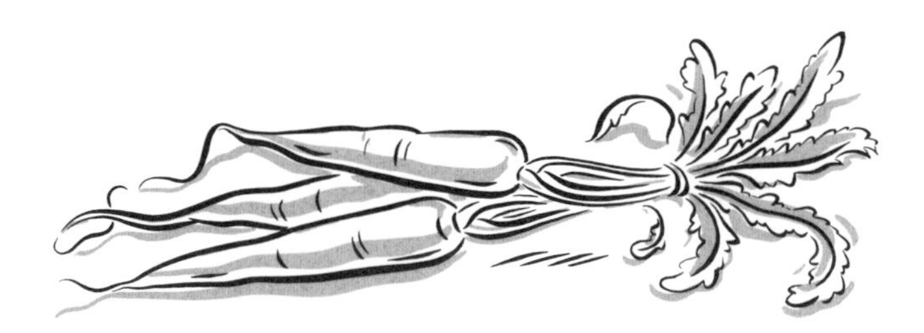

NUTRITION NOTE

It is a good idea to balance a diet which generally relies on meat or poultry for the main meal of the day by including some main dishes of vegetables and pulses on an occasional, but regular, basis. Mixed vegetable dishes with pulses are a good source of protein, particularly when served with grains or wholemeal bread.

Vegetable Chilli

FOOD VALUES	TOTAL	PER PORTION
Protein	59g	15g
Carbohydrate	203g	51g
Fat	58g	15g
Fibre	62g	16g
kcals	1518	380

1 *large aubergine, trimmed and cut into* 2.5 *cm/* 1 *inch cubes*
salt and pepper
60 *ml/*4 *tbsp oil*
1 *large onion, chopped*
4 *celery sticks, sliced*
1 *green pepper, seeded and chopped*
2 *garlic cloves, crushed*
1 *large potato, cut into* 2.5 *cm/*1 *inch cubes*
1 *large carrot, diced*
5-10 *ml/*1-2 *tsp chilli powder*
15 *ml/*1 *tbsp ground coriander*
15 *ml/*1 *tbsp ground cumin*
100 *g/*4 *oz mushrooms, sliced*
2 (397 *g/*14 *oz) cans chopped tomatoes*
2 (425 *g/*15 *oz) cans red kidney beans, drained*
2 *courgettes, halved lengthways and cut into chunks*
100 *g/*4 *oz frozen cut green beans or peas*

Place the aubergine cubes in a colander, sprinkling each layer with salt. Stand the colander over a bowl or in the sink and leave for 30 minutes. Rinse the aubergine and pat the cubes dry on absorbent kitchen paper.

Heat the oil in a large saucepan and fry the onion, celery, pepper and garlic until the onion is slightly softened. Stir in the aubergine and cook, stirring, until the outside of the cubes are lightly cooked. Stir in the potato, carrot, chilli, coriander and cumin. Stir for a few minutes to coat all the vegetables in the spices, then lightly mix in the mushrooms and tomatoes. Bring to the boil, lower the heat so that the mixture simmers and cover. Cook, stirring occasionally, for 30 minutes.

Add the kidney beans, courgettes, beans or peas, with salt and pepper to taste. Cover and continue to cook for a further 30 minutes, stirring occasionally, or until all the vegetables are tender. The juice from the vegetables, combined with the canned tomatoes, should be sufficient to keep the mixture moist. If the mixture cooks too quickly the liquid will evaporate and the vegetables may stick to the pan.

SERVES 4

COOK AHEAD FOR MID-WEEK

A PRACTICAL APPROACH TO COOKING AHEAD

There are a few ways in which main dishes can be prepared ahead – by batch baking large quantities and freezing them in useful-sized portions, by making double the quantity required for one meal and reserving the remainder for another planned meal within the next day or two, or by making dishes for specific meals and freezing or chilling them until required. Important points on food safety are outlined in the feature on Cook-Ahead Sense (page 73).

Dishes which can be cooked ahead successfully are those which do not taste inferior when reheated, and recipes which can be served in many ways are excellent candidates for everyday meals. Remember to consider the texture of cooked dishes as well as the flavour when you plan on cooking and reheating them. Homely soups can be varied according to the vegetables in season; they can be pepped up by adding a little curry spice or made extremely satisfying by adding a little pearl barley, rice or soup pasta.

Stews and sauces can be served in different ways to make a variety of meals. They can be ladled over rice or other grains and pasta, spooned into split baked potatoes or served with cooked seasonal vegetables. They can also be used to fill a pastry-topped or potato-covered pie; topped with a savoury crumble mixture; rolled into cooked pancakes and coated with a cheese or tomato sauce; or layered with cooked pasta, topped with cheese and baked until golden. Complete a menu based on a reheated main dish by serving plenty of fresh vegetables or a generous side salad which can be quite simple but nutritious. Fresh fruit for dessert will bring the meal to a healthy end.

Chicken Stock

Always use the leftovers from a roast chicken to make a good stock and freeze it if you do not have immediate use for it. If you do not have the time to make stock from the leftovers but do not want to throw them away, break up the bones and freeze them, then make the stock within a few days.

4 chicken drumsticks or 1 meaty chicken carcass
1 small onion, sliced
1 carrot, roughly chopped
1 celery stick, sliced
1 bouquet garni
5 ml/1 tsp white peppercorns

Break or chop the carcass into manageable pieces. Put it in a large saucepan with 1.75 litres/3 pints cold water. Bring to the boil; skim the surface. Add the remaining ingredients, lower the heat and simmer for 3-4 hours. Cool quickly, then strain. Skim off surface fat. Use as required.

MAKES ABOUT 1.4 LITRES/2½ PINTS

Vegetable Stock

Vary the vegetables according to the market selection and your personal taste. The nutrient content of stock in terms of the food values given is negligible.

2 onions, sliced
2 leeks, trimmed, sliced and washed
1 small turnip, chopped
4 celery sticks, sliced
2 tomatoes, chopped
1 bouquet garni
6 black peppercorns
2 cloves
a few lettuce leaves
a few spinach leaves
a few watercress sprigs
2.5 ml/½ tsp yeast extract (optional)
salt

Put the root vegetables, celery, tomatoes, herbs and spices in a large saucepan. Add 2 litres/3½ pints water. Bring to the boil, lower the heat and simmer for 1 hour.

Add the lettuce, spinach and watercress and simmer for 1 hour more. Stir in the yeast extract, if using, and add salt to taste. Strain the stock and use as required.

MAKES ABOUT 1.75 LITRES/3 PINTS

NUTRITION NOTE

Food values are not included for the stock recipes as they do not contain significant quantities of these nutrients.

Mixed Vegetable Soup

FOOD VALUES	TOTAL	PER PORTION
Protein	21g	4g
Carbohydrate	163g	27g
Fat	28g	5g
Fibre	38g	6g
kcals	951	159

30 *ml/2 tbsp oil*
1 *onion, chopped*
2 *leeks, trimmed, sliced and washed*
3 *celery sticks, sliced*
2 *potatoes, diced*
2 *carrots, diced*
1 *swede, diced*
1 *parsnip, diced*
1.75 *litres/3 pints Chicken Stock (page* 64) *or Vegetable Stock (page* 65)
salt and pepper

Heat the oil in a large, heavy-bottomed saucepan. Add the onion and leeks, and cook gently for 10 minutes, stirring occasionally. Add the remaining vegetables, pour in the stock and add salt and pepper to taste. Bring to the boil, lower the heat and cover the pan. Simmer for about 1 hour or until all the vegetables are tender and the soup is well flavoured.

If a clear soup with identifiable vegetables is preferred, serve at once. To thicken the soup, purée it in a blender or food processor, and return it to the pan.

SERVES 6

PRESSURE COOKER TIP

Put the vegetables for Mixed Vegetable Soup in the cooker with only 1 litre/1¾ pints of stock; the cooker should not be more than half full. Put the lid on the cooker and bring to 15 lb pressure. Cook for 5 minutes. Reduce pressure quickly. Add more stock if liked.

Minestrone can also be made in the pressure cooker. Make as suggested, but do not add the cabbage with the other vegetables. Reduce the quantity of stock to 900 ml/1½ pints. Put the lid on and bring to 15 lb pressure. Cook for 10 minutes; reduce the pressure slowly. Add the cabbage and pasta, stirring well. Close the lid again, bring back to 15 lb pressure and cook for 5 minutes more. Reduce the pressure slowly.

Minestrone

FOOD VALUES	TOTAL	PER PORTION
Protein	40g	7g
Carbohydrate	142g	24g
Fat	47g	8g
Fibre	25g	4g
kcals	1119	187

75 g/3 oz small haricot beans, soaked overnight in water to cover
15 ml/1 tbsp oil
2 rindless streaky bacon rashers, chopped
1 leek, trimmed, thinly sliced and washed
1 onion, chopped
1 garlic clove, crushed
2 carrots, thinly sliced
50 g/2 oz French beans, sliced
3 celery sticks, sliced
2 potatoes, diced
150 g/5 oz white cabbage, shredded
1 bay leaf
30 ml/2 tbsp tomato purée
1.25 litres/2¼ pints Chicken Stock (page 64)
salt and pepper
50 g/2 oz small pasta shells or rings
grated Parmesan cheese to serve

Drain the beans. Put them in a saucepan with fresh water to cover. Bring to the boil, boil vigorously for 10 minutes, then drain thoroughly.

Heat the oil in a large saucepan, add the bacon, leek, onion and garlic and fry gently for about 10 minutes. Add the remaining vegetables and cook, stirring frequently, for 2-3 minutes. Stir in the drained beans, with the bay leaf, tomato purée, stock and pepper. Do not add salt at this stage. Bring the soup to the boil, lower the heat, cover the pan and simmer for 45-60 minutes or until the haricot beans are tender. Add salt to taste.

Stir in the pasta and cook for 8-12 minutes or until tender but still firm to the bite. Remove the bay leaf. Serve the soup at once, sprinkled with Parmesan cheese.

SERVES 6

NUTRITION NOTE

Minestrone is satisfying, delicious and extremely well balanced. The beans and pasta provide plenty of carbohydrate and the beans are also a good source of protein.

Hodge-Podge

As the title suggests, this is a versatile soup which can be varied according to the ingredients available, particularly the vegetables. Cabbage, Brussels sprouts, cauliflower, celeriac and potatoes may all be added.

FOOD VALUES	TOTAL	PER PORTION
Protein	146g	24g
Carbohydrate	40g	7g
Fat	68g	11g
Fibre	9g	2g
kcals	1410	234

450 g/1 lb shin of beef, diced
300 ml/½ pint bitter beer or mild ale
2 onions, chopped
2 carrots, diced
2 turnips, diced
1 head of celery, sliced
salt and pepper
40 g/1½ oz butter
25 g/1 oz plain flour

Place the beef, beer and 1.25 litres/2¼ pints water in a large saucepan and bring to the boil. Skim the surface, then add the vegetables and plenty of seasoning. Reduce the heat and cover the pan. Simmer gently for 3 hours, until the meat is thoroughly tender.

Cream the butter and flour to a paste. Stir into the soup and bring to the boil. Simmer for 3 minutes, check the seasoning and serve.

SERVES 6

Yellow Split Pea Soup

FOOD VALUES	TOTAL	PER PORTION (6)
Protein	35g	6g
Carbohydrate	32g	5g
Fat	61g	10g
Fibre	5g	1g
kcals	810	135

30 ml/2 tbsp oil
6 rindless streaky bacon rashers, chopped
1 large onion, finely chopped
100 g/4 oz yellow split peas, soaked overnight in water to cover
2 litres/3½ pints Chicken Stock (page 64) or Vegetable Stock (page 65)
60 ml/4 tbsp chopped celery leaves
2 parsley sprigs
2 bay leaves
5 ml/1 tsp chopped summer savory or 2.5 ml/½ tsp dried savory
salt and pepper

Heat the oil in a large saucepan. Add the bacon and onion. Fry for 10 minutes over gentle heat, until the onion is soft but not coloured.

Drain the split peas and add them to the pan with the stock, celery leaves, parsley, bay leaves and savory. Add salt and pepper to taste. Bring to the boil, lower the heat and simmer for about 2 hours, or until the peas are very tender. If the soup becomes too thick, add water or extra stock.

Remove the parsley sprigs and bay leaves. Serve the soup as it is, or purée in a blender or food processor. Alternatively, rub through a sieve into a clean pan. Reheat, stirring frequently to prevent the soup from sticking to the pan, and serve at once.

SERVES 4 TO 6

PRESSURE COOKER TIP

It is not necessary to soak the split peas if the soup is to be made in a pressure cooker. Fry the bacon and onion in the oil in the open cooker. Add the split peas and herbs as in the recipe above, but reduce the amount of stock to 1 litre/1¾ pints. Put the lid on the cooker and bring to 15 lb pressure. Cook for 12 minutes. Reduce pressure slowly, then continue as described above, adding more stock to adjust the consistency as desired.

Beef and Bean Stew

Stews and casseroles improve if cooked a day ahead. Cool the cooked stew as quickly as possible, cover and store in the refrigerator. Next day, remove any fat from the surface of the stew and reheat on top of the stove or in the oven at 180°C/350°F/gas 4.

FOOD VALUES	TOTAL	PER PORTION
Protein	230g	38g
Carbohydrate	57g	10g
Fat	117g	20g
Fibre	8g	1g
kcals	2190	365

675 g/1½ lb leg of beef, trimmed and cut in neat 2cm/¾ inch thick pieces
seasoned flour
60 ml/4 tbsp oil
1 large onion, chopped
2 carrots, chopped
1 small turnip, chopped
750 ml/1¼ pints beef stock
30 ml/2 tbsp tomato purée
salt and pepper
75 g/3 oz haricot beans, soaked in water overnight
100 g/4 oz mushrooms, sliced

Toss the beef cubes in seasoned flour until well coated. The easiest way to do this is in a tightly closed stout polythene bag.

Heat the oil in a flameproof casserole and fry the onion, carrots and turnip until golden. With a slotted spoon, transfer the vegetables to a bowl and set aside. Add the floured beef cubes to the fat remaining in the pan and cook until browned on all sides. Pour off any excess fat and return the partially cooked vegetables to the pan. Gradually stir in the stock and tomato purée, with salt and pepper to taste. Simmer.

Drain the beans and place them in a separate saucepan with cold water to cover. Bring to the boil, boil vigorously for 10 minutes, then drain. Add the beans to the stew and simmer gently for about 2-2½ hours or until the meat and beans are tender. Stir occasionally during cooking, never allowing the liquid to boil as this will toughen the meat.

Add the mushrooms and cook for 20-30 minutes more. Serve at once, or transfer to a suitable container and cool, chill and refrigerate.

SERVES 6

Goulash

It is the paprika that gives this hearty Hungarian stew its delicious flavour. Serve simply, with pasta or crusty bread and a large bowl of mixed salad. Do not add the potatoes before freezing the goulash. Cook them separately in boiling water for 10 minutes, then drain and add them to the thawed stew. Simmer for a further 10 minutes before serving.

FOOD VALUES	TOTAL	PER PORTION
Protein	239g	40g
Carbohydrate	139g	23g
Fat	107g	18g
Fibre	11g	2g
kcals	2529	422

30 ml/2 tbsp oil
675 g/1½ lb chuck or blade steak, trimmed and cut into 2 cm/¾ inch cubes
2 onions, sliced
30 ml/2 tbsp plain flour
125 ml/4 fl oz beef stock
125 ml/4 fl oz red wine
450 g/1 lb tomatoes, peeled and diced or 1 (397 g/14 oz) can chopped tomatoes
2.5 ml/½ tsp salt
15 ml/1 tbsp paprika
1 bouquet garni
450 g/1 lb potatoes
150 ml/¼ pint fromage frais or plain yogurt

Heat the oil in a flameproof casserole and fry the meat until browned on all sides. Using a slotted spoon, remove the meat and set aside. Add the onions to the fat remaining in the casserole and fry gently until just beginning to brown. Add the flour and cook, stirring until browned.

Gradually add the stock and wine, with the tomatoes, salt, paprika and bouquet garni. Bring just to the boil, stirring, then lower the heat and simmer for 1-2 hours or until the meat is tender. Alternatively, transfer the goulash to a casserole and bake at 160°C/325°F/gas 3 for 1½-2 hours.

Thirty minutes before the end of the cooking time, peel the potatoes, cut them into cubes and add them to the goulash. When cooked they should be tender but not broken. Just before serving, remove the bouquet garni and stir in the fromage frais or yogurt.

SERVES 6

Bologneѕe Sauce

This sauce is enriched by the addition of chicken livers and a little wine. Serve with spaghetti or pasta shapes and a simple side salad. The meat sauce is also good ladled into baked potatoes or served with rice.

FOOD VALUES	TOTAL	PER PORTION
Protein	91g	23g
Carbohydrate	27g	7g
Fat	103g	26g
Fibre	6g	2g
kcals	1472	368

15 ml/1 tbsp olive oil
75 g/3 oz unsmoked rindless streaky bacon rashers, diced
1 onion, finely chopped
2 garlic cloves, crushed
1 carrot, finely diced
1 celery stick, thinly sliced
225 g/8 oz lean minced beef
100 g/4 oz chicken livers, trimmed and cut into small shreds
1 (397 g/14 oz) can chopped tomatoes
200 ml/7 fl oz beef stock
15 ml/1 tbsp tomato purée
125 ml/4 fl oz dry white or red wine
5 ml/1 tsp dried marjoram
salt and pepper
pinch of grated nutmeg

Heat the oil in a saucepan. Add the bacon and cook it gently until brown. Add the onion, garlic, carrot and celery. Cook over gentle heat for about 10 minutes until the onion is soft and just beginning to brown. Add the beef and cook, stirring, until browned and broken up.

Add the chicken livers to the pan and cook for 3 minutes, turning the livers over gently to brown them on all sides. Stir in the tomatoes, stock, tomato purée, wine and marjoram. Add salt, pepper and nutmeg to taste. Bring to simmering point and cook, covered, for about 1 hour, stirring occasionally.

Remove the lid for the final 20 minutes of the cooking time to allow some of the liquid to evaporate. Taste and add extra salt and pepper if necessary.

SERVES 4

COOK AHEAD SENSE

If you have sufficient refrigerator space or a freezer, it makes good sense to prepare some dishes in larger quantities for freezing or to plan ahead for days when you know you will have little time to spare for preparing meals. There are a few points to remember to ensure that the cooked dishes taste as good when they are reheated and served as they did when they were first cooked. These simple rules also avoid any risk of food poisoning from cooking ahead and reheating.

COOK AND CHILL REMINDERS

Here are a few food-hygiene reminders for cooling, storing and reheating dishes which you keep chilled rather than frozen.

- Cook dishes which you intend to use within the next one or two days – as a rule, do not prepare dishes more than two days ahead.
- Transfer the cooked food promptly to a clean container and cover it, then leave to cool. Do not leave foods such as soups and stews in their cooking dishes as it takes longer for the food to cool down.
- As soon as the food is cool place it in the refrigerator and keep it chilled until you are ready to reheat and serve it.
- Foods which are served cold (such as cooked ham, meatloaf and so on) should be removed from the refrigerator just before serving, the required portions removed and any leftovers replaced.
- Thoroughly reheat food to be served hot just before serving. Stir or rearrange the food to ensure it is completely and evenly heated to the original cooking temperature. Do not serve food warm. Serve the food promptly after reheating.
- Never leave food to stand uncovered.
- Do not reheat food more than once. Some foods, such as a vegetable soup which may be boiled, may be reheated twice but this is not ideal as the process of cooling and reheating encourages micro-organisms in the food to multiply.

FREEZING, THAWING AND USING COOKED DISHES

Cool and freeze the food as soon as possible after cooking. Add rice, pasta or potatoes to soups and similar dishes with a high proportion of liquid after thawing. If you intend freezing cooked dishes for more than a week or two, use garlic, herbs and spices with care, as flavours can deteriorate or mature.

Pack cooked foods in freezer containers, or in ordinary dishes which will withstand freezing and heating. Label carefully if additional ingredients have to be included during re-heating. Use cooked foods within 2 months to retain high quality. Thaw all dishes and make sure they are thoroughly reheated to the original cooking temperature.

The safest way to thaw food is to unwrap it and place it in a covered container in the refrigerator overnight. The important point to remember is that as the food thaws, the bacteria and enzymes contained in it slowly become active as the temperature rises. While the food remains very cold there is no risk of it being open to contamination by bacterial growth; however if the food is left in a warm room for a long period, parts, if not all, of it will become sufficiently warm for bacteria to grow. Foods left in this manner for long periods may develop high levels of bacteria with the possible consequence of food poisoning. It is therefore vital that food thawed at room temperature should be frequently monitored. It should be used as soon as it is thawed, while still very cold.

Keep a record of the contents of your freezer and update it regularly.

- Move items to be used promptly to the top or front of the freezer.
- Freeze food which is in good condition and produce in its prime.
- Before you freeze food, always consider how you intend using it.
- Pack all food in sealed containers or bags.
- Exclude as much air as possible from packs except when freezing liquid items which require headspace to allow for expansion.
- Always label packs – even though the contents may be evident when fresh, they will be far more difficult to identify when frozen.

FOOD STORAGE CONTAINERS

Cooked food which is not served straight away should be transferred to a clean container promptly after cooking. If hot dishes, such as casseroles and stews, are left in the cooking container, they take longer to cool. Many top-quality plastic storage containers withstand the temperature of hot sauces and stews which have been allowed to stand for about 15 minutes after cooking. However, less-expensive plastic containers are not suitable for holding hot food.

There is a wide variety of dishes which are suitable for use in the freezer, oven or for serving food but it is not always practical to keep them in the freezer for long periods. Line the container with a polythene freezer bag, then fill it with the food, seal and place it in the freezer. Once the food is firm, remove the bag from the dish for storage.

Remember that it is equally important to make sure food is properly packed when it is stored in the refrigerator as well as in the freezer. Many dishes with lids are not practical as they take up too much space. Cling film may be used to cover food tightly instead of using a loose-fitting lid. Always make sure that the container is large enough to retain all the juices and that it has a flat base to stand firmly on the wire shelves in the refrigerator, so avoiding any chance of tilting the dish and spilling the food. Polythene food bags are ideal for use in the refrigerator but they are not thick enough to provide adequate protection when freezing food.

TEMPERATURE CHECK

The refrigerator should have an internal temperature of 5°C/41°F or less and the freezer should have an internal temperature of −18°C/0°F or less. It is a good idea to buy a purpose-made thermometer to check.

COOKED DISHES FREEZING CHART

Type of dish	Preparation for freezing	High quality storage life
Casseroles and stews	Slightly undercook vegetables. Do not add rice, pasta or potatoes. Remove surplus fat.	2 months
Flans (sweet and savoury)	Prepare and bake. Open freeze, then wrap.	2 months
Meat	Do not freeze cooked joints or grilled meats; they can become tough, rancid and dry. Slice cooked meat thinly and pack in sauce or gravy.	2 months
Meat pies	**1** Bake and cool. Wrap. **2** Cook meat filling. Cool and cover with pastry.	**1** 2 months **2** 2 months
Mousses	Prepare in freezer-tested serving dishes.	1 month
Pancakes	Cool and pack in layers with interleaving film.	2 months
Pasta dishes	Pack pasta and sauce in foil dish with lid.	1 month
Pâté	Cool completely and wrap.	1 month
Pizza	Bake. Cool and wrap. Alternatively, par-bake base, then add topping and freeze.	1 month
Rice	Slightly undercook, drain well, cool, and pack.	1 month
Sauces (savoury)	Prepare completely, but season sparingly. Pack in rigid containers, leaving headspace. *Do not freeze sauces thickened with eggs or cream.*	1 month
Sauces (sweet)	**1** Fresh or cooked fruit sauces should be packed in rigid containers, leaving headspace. **2** Thicken pudding sauces with cornflour and pack in rigid containers, leaving headspace. *Do not freeze custard sauces.*	**1** 12 months **2** 1 month
Soups	Do not include rice, pasta, barley, potatoes, milk, cream or eggs. Pack in rigid containers, leaving neadspace.	2 months
Steamed and baked puddings	Steam or bake puddings in foil containers. Cool and cover.	2 months

Chilli Con Carne

FOOD VALUES	TOTAL	PER PORTION
Protein	189g	47g
Carbohydrate	78g	20g
Fat	171g	43g
Fibre	27g	7g
kcals	2590	648

225 g/8 oz red kidney beans, soaked overnight in water to cover
225 g/8 oz rindless smoked streaky bacon rashers, chopped
1 Spanish onion, chopped
2 garlic cloves, crushed
30 ml/2 tbsp ground coriander
15 ml/1 tbsp ground cumin
15 ml/1 tbsp chilli powder or to taste
450 g/1 lb minced beef
1 beef stock cube
30 ml/2 tbsp tomato purée
salt and pepper
30 ml/2 tbsp chopped fresh coriander or parsley

Drain the beans and put them in a large saucepan. Add plenty of water and bring to the boil. Boil vigorously for 10 minutes, then lower the heat, cover the pan and simmer gently for 30 minutes.

Put the bacon in a large heavy-bottomed saucepan. Heat gently until the fat runs. Add the onion and fry, stirring frequently for about 5 minutes until the onion is soft but not browned. Stir in the garlic, ground coriander, cumin and chilli powder. Cook for 1 minute, stirring, then add the meat and cook until lightly browned. Crumble in the stock cube and pour in 600 ml/1 pint water. Stir in the tomato purée and add salt and pepper to taste. Bring to the boil.

Drain the beans. Add them to the saucepan and bring the stock back to the boil. Cover the pan, lower the heat and simmer gently for about 1 hour or until the beans are tender and the liquid has been absorbed. Stir in the coriander or parsley. Serve at once, with rice, crusty bread or as a filling for baked jacket potatoes.

SERVES 4

NUTRITION NOTE

Chilli con carne is satisfying and nutritious, with plenty of protein from the meat and beans. The beans also contribute fibre. Buy lean minced beef or dry fry it separately first, then use a slotted spoon to remove the meat from the pan and drain away the fat which the meat yields.

Cottage Pie

Potatoes make a significant contribution to the diet, not only for the energy they provide but also as a valuable source of vitamin C when eaten frequently.

FOOD VALUES	TOTAL	PER PORTION (6)
Protein	156g	26g
Carbohydrate	184g	31g
Fat	137g	23g
Fibre	17g	3g
kcals	2547	425

15 ml/1 tbsp oil
575 g/1¼ lb minced beef
1 onion, chopped
2 carrots, finely chopped
100 g/4 oz mushrooms, chopped
30 ml/2 tbsp plain flour
300 ml/½ pint beef stock
5 ml/1 tsp Worcestershire sauce
salt and pepper
900 g/2 lb potatoes, halved
25 g/1 oz butter or margarine
30 ml/2 tbsp milk
pinch of grated nutmeg

Heat the oil in a saucepan and fry the minced beef until browned, stirring to break up any lumps. Add the chopped onion, carrots and mushrooms and cook for 10 minutes or until softened slightly. Stir in the flour, then pour in the beef stock and Worcestershire sauce, with salt and pepper to taste. Bring to the boil, stirring, then cover the pan and simmer for 30 minutes.

Cook the potatoes in boiling water for about 20 minutes or until tender. Drain thoroughly and mash with a potato masher. Beat in the butter or margarine and the milk to make a creamy consistency. Add salt, pepper and nutmeg to taste.

Set the oven at 200°C/400°F/gas 6. Spoon the meat mixture into an ovenproof dish. Cover with the potato and mark the top with a fork. Bake for about 25 minutes until the potato topping is browned.

SERVES 4 TO 6

Beef Galantine

The browned breadcrumbs improve the appearance of the galantine which tastes far better than it looks. It is very similar to corned beef in flavour – ideal for sandwiches or to serve with salad or baked beans and baked potatoes.

FOOD VALUES	TOTAL	PER PORTION (6)
Protein	228g	38g
Carbohydrate	91g	15g
Fat	119g	17g
Fibre	3g	1g
kcals	2323	388

200 g/7 oz lean rindless back bacon, minced
450 g/1 lb chuck or blade steak, minced
150 g/5 oz fresh breadcrumbs
salt and pepper
1 egg, beaten
75 ml/3 fl oz beef stock
60 ml/4 tbsp browned breadcrumbs
oil for greasing

The galantine may either be steamed or boiled in stock. If the former, prepare a steamer. Alternatively, half fill a large saucepan with stock and bring to the boil.

Combine the bacon, meat and breadcrumbs in a bowl. Add salt and pepper to taste and mix together well. Mix the egg and measured stock together and combine this thoroughly with the meat mixture. Shape into a short, thick roll, then wrap in greased greaseproof paper. Wrap in a scalded pudding cloth or foil, tying or twisting the ends securely.
Put the roll on the perforated part of the steamer, curving it round if necessary, and steam for 2 hours, or lower it gently into the fast-boiling stock, lower the heat and simmer for 2 hours. Check the volume of water frequently if using a steamer, and top it up with boiling water from a kettle as necessary.

When cooked, lift out the roll, unwrap it, and then roll up tightly in a clean dry pudding cloth. Press the roll between two plates until just cold. Then remove the cloth, roll the meat in the browned breadcrumbs; chill until ready to serve.

SERVES 6 TO 8

LIGHT DISHES FOR LUNCH OR SUPPER

Bread Soup

Originally intended for times when extreme economy was the object, this version with vegetables is satisfying and tasty.

FOOD VALUES	TOTAL	PER PORTION
Protein	10g	3g
Carbohydrate	61g	15g
Fat	23g	6g
Fibre	6g	2g
kcals	476	119

40 g/1½ oz butter
2 onions, chopped
100 g/4 oz fresh breadcrumbs
2 carrots, diced
1 bay leaf
1.1 litres/2 pints Chicken Stock (page 64)
60 ml/4 tbsp chopped parsley
salt and pepper
grated nutmeg

Melt the butter in a large saucepan. Add the onions and fry for 10 minutes without browning. Add the breadcrumbs and cook, stirring, for 5 minutes, then add all the remaining ingredients.

Bring to the boil, reduce the heat and cover the pan. Simmer for 45 minutes. Taste for seasoning, then serve piping hot.

SERVES 4

French Onion Soup

FOOD VALUES	TOTAL	PER PORTION
Protein	58g	15g
Carbohydrate	267g	67g
Fat	89g	22g
Fibre	14g	4g
kcals	2047	512

25 g/1 oz butter
6 onions, about 575 g/ 1¼ lb, thinly sliced
1 litre/1¾ pints beef stock
30 ml/2 tbsp dry white wine
salt and pepper
6 slices of French bread
50 g/2 oz Gruyère, grated

Melt the butter in a large heavy-bottomed saucepan. Add the onions and cook slowly, turning occasionally, for at least 30 minutes, or until golden brown.

Stir in the stock and white wine. Bring to the boil, lower the heat and cover the pan, then simmer for about 1 hour, or until the onions are quite soft. Add salt and pepper to taste.

Toast the French bread and top it with grated cheese. Pour the soup into individual bowls, float a slice of toast on each, and brown the cheese under a preheated hot grill or in a very hot oven.

SERVES 4

MRS BEETON'S TIP

Sprinkle 2.5 ml/½ tsp sugar over the onions while browning them in the butter. This will encourage the browning process.

Leek and Oat Broth

FOOD VALUES	TOTAL	PER PORTION
Protein	23g	6g
Carbohydrate	50g	13g
Fat	6g	2g
Fibre	13g	3g
kcals	336	84

1 litre/1¾ pints Chicken Stock (*page* 64)
3 leeks, trimmed, sliced and washed
1 bay leaf
salt and pepper
60 ml/4 tbsp fine or medium oatmeal
150 ml/¼ pint reduced-fat single cream or fromage frais

Bring the stock and leeks to the boil in a large saucepan. Add the bay leaf and salt and pepper to taste. Lower the heat and simmer for 20 minutes.

Sprinkle the oatmeal into the simmering soup, whisking all the time and simmer for 5 minutes more. Then cover and simmer gently for a further 15-20 minutes, until thickened. Stir in the cream or fromage frais, reheat without boiling and serve.

SERVES 4

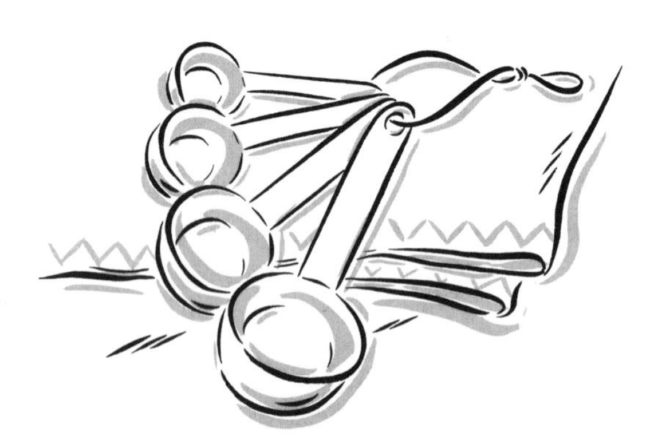

NUTRITION NOTE

Reduced-fat cream and vegetable-based cream substitutes are useful alternatives to ordinary single or double cream. Plain yogurt and fromage frais are also practical alternatives. Quick-cook porridge oats may be substituted for oatmeal and the soup simmered for just 5 minutes before adding the cream or fromage frais.

Smoked Mackerel Pâté

Omitting lemon juice from recipes such as this which traditionally call for cream and substituting plain yogurt for the cream usually results in a good balance of flavours.

FOOD VALUES	TOTAL	PER PORTION
Protein	93g	16g
Carbohydrate	24g	4g
Fat	160g	27g
Fibre	3g	–
kcals	1900	317

25 g/1 oz butter
2 shallots, finely chopped
75 g/3 oz tomato purée
5 ml/1 tsp soft light brown sugar
8 crushed peppercorns
15 ml/1 tbsp shredded fresh basil
1.25 ml/¼ tsp dried tarragon
few drops of Tabasco sauce (optional)
450 g/1 lb smoked mackerel fillets, skinned
75 ml/5 tbsp plain yogurt

Melt the butter in a saucepan, add the shallots and cook over gentle heat for 2-3 minutes until soft. Add the tomato purée, sugar, peppercorns and herbs, and cook gently for 4-5 minutes. Stir in the Tabasco sauce (if used), then set aside to cool slightly.

Roughly purée the shallot mixture, mackerel fillets and yogurt in a blender or food processor. Turn into a suitable dish and cool. Cover and chill until firm. Serve with toast.

SERVES 6

Spicy Fish Slices

Inexpensive coley or rather bland whiting fillets may also be used in this recipe. Rich mackerel fillets also taste good when cooked with spices; however, remember that oily fish has a far higher fat content than white fish.

FOOD VALUES	TOTAL	PER PORTION (4)
Protein	141g	35g
Carbohydrate	–	–
Fat	50g	13g
Fibre	–	–
kcals	1001	250

675 g/1½ lb cod, haddock or hake fillets
salt
5 ml/1 tsp turmeric
5 ml/1 tsp chilli powder
45 ml/3 tbsp oil
fresh coriander sprigs to garnish

Cut the fish into 2 cm/¾ inch slices and spread these out in a shallow dish large enough to hold all the slices in a single layer. Mix the salt and spices in a bowl. Stir in enough water to make a thick paste. Rub the paste into the fish, cover and leave to marinate for 1 hour.

Heat the oil in a large frying pan. Add as much of the spiced fish as possible, but do not overfill the pan. Fry the fish for 5-10 minutes until golden brown all over, then remove from the pan with a slotted spoon. Drain on absorbent kitchen paper and keep hot while cooking the rest of the fish. Garnish and serve hot, with rice and a salad.

SERVES 4 TO 5

Grilled Smoked Haddock

Poached eggs may be served with grilled or poached smoked haddock. Wholemeal bread, thinly spread with butter is the ideal accompaniment.

FOOD VALUES	TOTAL	PER PORTION
Protein	105g	26g
Carbohydrate	–	–
Fat	45g	11g
Fibre	–	–
kcals	823	206

450-575 *g/1-1¼ lb smoked haddock fillet, trimmed and cut into serving portions*
melted butter or oil for brushing
½ *lemon, cut into wedges*
freshly ground black pepper

Place the fish in a large frying pan and pour in boiling water to cover. Leave to stand for 5 minutes. Carefully remove each portion with a fish slice, drain well and arrange, skin side up, in a grill pan.

Grill under moderate heat for 3-5 minutes, depending on the thickness of the fish. Turn the fish over, brush the uncooked sides with melted butter or oil and grill for 4 minutes more.

Serve on warmed plates with lemon wedges and freshly ground black pepper. The juice from the lemon is squeezed over the haddock and pepper added to taste.

SERVES 4

Grilled Kippers

FOOD VALUES	TOTAL	PER PORTION
Protein	172g	43g
Carbohydrate	–	–
Fat	126g	32g
Fibre	–	–
kcals	1826	457

4 kippers
20 ml/4 tsp butter
chopped parsley to garnish

Lay the kippers flat, skin side up, in the base of the grill pan. Do not place on a rack. Grill under moderate heat for 3 minutes.

Turn the kippers over, dot each one with 5 ml/1 tsp butter and grill for 3 minutes more. Serve on warmed plates, topping each portion with a sprinkling of chopped parsley.

SERVES 4

MRS BEETON'S TIP

An alternative, traditional, method of preparing kippers is to 'jug' them. Put the kippers, tail ends up, in a tall heatproof jug. Then pour freshly boiling water from the kettle into the jug to cover all but the tails of the fish. Cover the jug with a clean cloth and leave to stand for 5 minutes. Tilt the jug gently over a sink and drain off the water – do not attempt to pull the kippers out by their tails as they may disintergrate. Serve at once on warm plates, with lemon wedges and parsley.

Tuna Sauce

Serve with cooked pasta or rice. The sauce may also be ladled into split baked potatoes or into scooped-out crusty rolls or lengths of warmed French bread.

FOOD VALUES	TOTAL	PER PORTION
Protein	80g	20g
Carbohydrate	49g	12g
Fat	57g	19g
Fibre	3g	1g
kcals	1020	253

25 *g*/1 *oz butter or margarine*
1 *onion, chopped*
25 *g*/1 *oz plain flour*
450 *ml*/¾ *pint milk*
100 *g*/4 *oz mushrooms, sliced*
50 *g*/2 *oz Cheddar cheese, grated*
salt and pepper
30 *ml*/2 *tbsp chopped parsley*
1 (200 *g*/7 *oz*) *can tuna in brine, drained and flaked*

Melt the butter or margarine in a saucepan. Add the onion and cook gently, stirring occasionally, for about 15 minutes or until soft. Stir in the flour and cook for 1 minute, then reduce the heat to low and slowly pour in the milk, stirring constantly. Bring to the boil, lower the heat again and simmer for 3 minutes.

Stir the mushrooms and cheese into the sauce with salt and pepper to taste. Cook over low heat until the cheese melts, then add the parsley and flaked drained tuna. Stir for 1-2 minutes until the tuna is hot. Serve at once.

SERVES 4

Chicken and Ham Gratins

FOOD VALUES	TOTAL	PER PORTION
Protein	95g	24g
Carbohydrate	48g	12g
Fat	72g	18g
Fibre	1g	–
kcals	1208	302

25 g/1 oz butter or margarine
25 g/1 oz plain flour
300 ml/½ pint milk, chicken stock or a mixture
250 g/9 oz boneless cooked chicken
100 g/4 oz cooked ham
salt and pepper
good pinch of grated nutmeg
60 ml/4 tbsp fine dried white breadcrumbs

Set the oven at 190-200°C/375-400°F/gas 5-6. Melt the butter or margarine in a saucepan. Stir in the flour and cook over low heat for 2-3 minutes, without colouring. Gradually add the liquid, stirring constantly. Bring to the boil, stirring, then simmer for 1-2 minutes until smooth and thickened. Add salt and pepper to taste. Cool.

Remove any skin from the chicken. Chop the meat coarsely and place in a bowl. Chop the ham finely and add it to the chicken. Moisten the mixture well with some of the sauce. Add salt and pepper to taste and a good pinch of grated nutmeg.

Divide the chicken mixture between four gratin dishes. Top with the remaining sauce, then sprinkle evenly with breadcrumbs. Bake for about 20 minutes, until golden brown.

SERVES 4

Kidneys in Italian Sauce

FOOD VALUES	TOTAL	PER PORTION
Protein	120g	30g
Carbohydrate	44g	11g
Fat	50g	13g
Fibre	5g	1g
kcals	1127	282

450 g/1 lb lambs' kidneys
45 ml/3 tbsp plain flour
salt and pepper
30 ml/2 tbsp olive oil
8 young fresh sage leaves (optional)
1 small onion, finely chopped
25 g/1 oz butter or margarine
375 ml/13 fl oz beef stock
100 g/4 oz mushrooms, sliced
15-30 ml/1-2 tbsp sherry

Wash the kidneys, halve and remove the membrane and white core from each. Cut into slices. Mix the flour with salt and pepper in a shallow bowl. Coat the kidneys in seasoned flour; shake off and reserve excess flour.

Heat the oil in a frying pan, add the kidney slices and sage, if using, and fry quickly, stirring, until firm. Add the onion, lower the heat, cover and fry gently for 20 minutes.

Meanwhile, melt the butter or margarine in a saucepan, stir in the reserved flour and cook until nut brown in colour. Gradually add the stock, stirring constantly, and bring to the boil. Lower the heat and simmer for 5 minutes.

With a slotted spoon, transfer the kidney slices and onions to the sauce. Half cover the pan and simmer the mixture for 4-5 minutes, then add the mushrooms and sherry, with extra salt and pepper if liked. Simmer for 15 minutes more. Serve with pasta, rice or baked potatoes.

SERVES 4

Devilled Kidneys

FOOD VALUES	TOTAL	PER PORTION
Protein	137g	34g
Carbohydrate	109g	27g
Fat	63g	13g
Fibre	4g	1g
kcals	1517	379

8 lambs' kidneys
30 ml/2 tbsp oil
15 ml/1 tbsp chopped onion
2.5 ml/½ tsp salt
1.25 ml/¼ tsp cayenne pepper
5 ml/1 tsp Worcestershire sauce
10 ml/2 tsp lemon juice
2.5 ml/½ tsp prepared mustard
125 ml/4 fl oz beef stock
2 egg yolks
fresh white breadcrumbs
wholemeal toast, to serve

Skin, halve and core the kidneys, then chop them into small pieces. Heat the oil in a small saucepan, add the onion and cook gently for 4-6 minutes until softened but not browned. Add the kidneys, salt, cayenne, Worcestershire sauce, lemon juice, mustard and stock. Bring to the boil, lower the heat and simmer for 15-20 minutes, until the kidneys are cooked. Cool slightly.

Beat the egg yolks lightly and stir them quickly into the kidney mixture. Sprinkle in enough of the breadcrumbs to give the mixture a soft consistency. Add more salt and pepper if required. Serve on wholemeal toast.

SERVES 4

Cauliflower Cheese

FOOD VALUES	TOTAL	PER PORTION
Protein	57g	19g
Carbohydrate	62g	16g
Fat	72g	18g
Fibre	8g	2g
kcals	1109	277

salt and pepper
1 firm cauliflower
30 ml/2 tbsp butter
60 ml/4 tbsp plain flour
200 ml/7 fl oz milk
100 g/4 oz Cheddar cheese, grated
pinch of dry mustard
pinch of cayenne pepper
25 g/1 oz dried white breadcrumbs

Bring a saucepan of water to the boil, add the cauliflower, cover the pan and cook gently for about 15 minutes until tender. Drain well, reserving 175 ml/6 fl oz of the cooking water. Place the whole cauliflower in a warmed ovenproof dish, cover and keep hot.

Set the oven at 220°C/425°F/gas 7 or preheat the grill. Melt the butter in a saucepan, stir in the flour and cook for 1 minute. Gradually add the milk and reserved cooking water, stirring all the time until the sauce boils and thickens. Remove from the heat and stir in most of the cheese, stirring until it melts into the sauce. Add the mustard and cayenne, with salt and pepper to taste.

Pour the sauce over the cauliflower. Mix the remaining cheese with the breadcrumbs and sprinkle them on top. Brown the topping for 7-10 minutes in the oven or under the grill. Serve at once.

SERVES 4

VARIATIONS

A wide variety of vegetables can be cooked in this way. Try broccoli (particularly good with grilled bacon); small whole onions; celery, celeriac; leeks or chicory (both taste delicious if wrapped in ham before being covered in the cheese sauce) and asparagus. A mixed vegetable gratin with cooked sliced carrots, green beans, onions and potatoes also works well.

Cauliflower and Cashew Nut Stir Fry

FOOD VALUES	TOTAL	PER PORTION (4)
Protein	25g	6g
Carbohydrate	26g	7g
Fat	49g	12g
Fibre	9g	3g
kcals	696	174

30 ml/2 tbsp oil
5 ml/1 tsp sesame oil (optional)
1 small cauliflower, broken into small florets
30 ml/2 tbsp grated fresh root ginger (optional)
1 bunch of spring onions, shredded
50 g/2 oz salted cashew nuts
5 ml/1 tsp cornflour
15 ml/1 tbsp soy sauce (optional, or salt to taste)
60 ml/4 tbsp dry sherry

Heat the oil in a large frying pan or wok. Add the sesame oil for a Chinese-style dish. Add the cauliflower and ginger – again for a Chinese flavour – and stir fry for 3 minutes. Add the spring onions and cashew nuts, then continue to cook for a further 3 minutes, until the cauliflower has lost its raw edge.

Blend the cornflour with the soy sauce, if you are opting for the Chinese flavour, otherwise add a little salt. In either case, stir in the sherry and 30 ml/ 2 tbsp water. Pour the cornflour mixture over the cauliflower and stir for 1-2 minutes, over high heat, until the juices thicken. Serve at once.

SERVES 4 TO 6

Stuffed Onions

FOOD VALUES	TOTAL	PER PORTION
Protein	56g	9g
Carbohydrate	86g	14g
Fat	60g	10g
Fibre	13g	2g
kcals	1081	180

salt and pepper
6 large onions
75 g/3 oz cooked ham, finely chopped
30 ml/2 tbsp fresh breadcrumbs
2.5 ml/½ tsp finely chopped sage
beaten egg for binding
30 ml/2 tbsp butter
100 g/4 oz Cheddar cheese, grated (optional)

Bring a saucepan of salted water to the boil, add the unpeeled onions and parboil for 4-5 minutes or until almost tender. Drain, skin and remove the centres with a teaspoon.

Set the oven at 180°C/350°F/gas 4. Mix the ham, breadcrumbs and sage in a small bowl. Add salt and pepper to taste and stir in enough of the beaten egg to give a fairly firm mixture. Fill the centres of the onions with the mixture. Put the onions in a baking dish just large enough to hold them snugly. Dot the tops with butter. Bake for 30-45 minutes or until tender, sprinkling the tops of the onions with the grated cheese, if used, 10 minutes before the end of the cooking time.

SERVES 6

MICROWAVE TIP

Peel the onions. Arrange them around the rim of a round shallow dish, add 45 ml/3 tbsp water and cover. Cook on High for 10-12 minutes or until the onions are tender. When cool enough to handle, scoop out the centres and fill as described above. Return the onions to the dry dish and cook for 4-6 minutes. If a cheese topping is required, sprinkle the grated cheese on top and brown under a grill for 3-4 minutes.

Cheese and Potato Pie

Serve a fresh salad to complement this plain, but quite rich, dish. Sliced tomatoes with onion on a generous bed of mixed salad leaves would be ideal. If you do not favour raw onion, add spring onion or slightly peppery watercress sprigs to give the meal a bit of bite. A tangy dressing of fresh orange juice makes a refreshing accompaniment.

FOOD VALUES	TOTAL	PER PORTION
Protein	58g	15g
Carbohydrate	117g	29g
Fat	63g	16g
Fibre	8g	2g
kcals	1240	310

fat for greasing
675 *g*/1½ *lb potatoes, halved*
175 *g*/6 *oz Cheddar cheese, finely grated*
salt and pepper
milk (see method)

Grease a pie dish. Cook the potatoes in a saucepan of boiling water for about 20 minutes or until tender. Drain thoroughly and mash until smooth.

Add 150 g/5 oz of the grated cheese, with salt and pepper to taste, then beat well with enough milk to make a creamy mixture. Spoon into the dish, sprinkle with the remaining cheese and brown under a moderate grill for 3-5 minutes. Serve at once.

SERVES 4

Macaroni Cheese

FOOD VALUES	TOTAL	PER PORTION (3)
Protein	61g	20g
Carbohydrate	134g	45g
Fat	93g	31g
Fibre	5g	2g
kcals	1583	528

150 g/5 oz elbow macaroni
salt and pepper
50 g/2 oz butter or margarine
50 g/2 oz plain flour
600 ml/1 pint milk, stock or a mixture
100 g/4 oz Cheddar cheese, grated

Set the oven at 200°C/400°F/gas 6. Cook the macaroni in a large saucepan of boiling salted water for 10-12 minutes or until tender but still firm to the bite.

Meanwhile, melt the butter or margarine in a saucepan. Stir in the flour and cook over low heat for 2-3 minutes without browning. Gradually pour in the milk or stock and bring to the boil, stirring constantly. Simmer for 2 minutes, stirring occasionally. Remove from the heat.

Drain the macaroni thoroughly and stir it gently into the white sauce. Add three-quarters of the cheese, with salt and pepper to taste. Spoon the mixture into an ovenproof dish. Sprinkle with the remaining cheese and bake for 15-20 minutes.

Alternatively, place under a preheated grill for 2-4 minutes to melt and brown the cheese topping.

SERVES 3 TO 4

NUTRITION NOTE

Pasta is a useful low-fat food for supper dishes and main meals. Use skimmed or semi-skimmed milk and low-fat cheeses in sauces to make low-fat dishes. Toss freshly cooked pasta with a little hot olive oil and garlic, then serve it with a large salad and bread for a supper which is rich in carbohydrate but low in saturated fats.

Creamed Pasta

FOOD VALUES	TOTAL	PER PORTION
Protein	63g	16g
Carbohydrate	17g	4g
Fat	96g	24g
Fibre	–	–
kcals	1177	294

175 *g*/6 *oz macaroni or tagliatelle*
300 *ml*/½ *pint milk*
300 *ml*/½ *pint Chicken Stock* (*page* 64) *or Vegetable Stock* (*page* 65)
3 *egg yolks*
salt and pepper
60 *ml*/4 *tbsp reduced-fat single cream, fromage frais or plain yogurt*
100 *g*/4 *oz Cheshire cheese, grated*

Place the pasta in a large saucepan with the milk and stock. Bring to the boil, stirring, reduce the heat so that the pasta simmers without boiling over and cover the pan. Simmer for 20 minutes, or until the pasta is tender. Stir occasionally to prevent the pasta from sticking.

Drain the pasta, reserving the cooking liquid, and place in a flameproof serving dish. Return the liquid to the pan. Beat the egg yolks, seasoning and cream, fromage frais or yogurt. Pour this into the liquid in the pan and heat gently without boiling. Stir in most of the cheese and pour over the pasta. Toss well and sprinkle with the remaining cheese. Brown under a hot grill and serve at once.

SERVES 4

Cheese Pudding

FOOD VALUES	TOTAL	PER PORTION
Protein	70g	18g
Carbohydrate	61g	15g
Fat	76g	19g
Fibre	2g	1g
kcals	1194	299

fat for greasing
100-150 *g/4-5 oz Cheddar or Gruyère cheese, grated*
2 *eggs, beaten*
250 *ml/8 fl oz whole or skimmed milk*
100 *g/4 oz fresh breadcrumbs*
salt (optional)

Butter an ovenproof dish. Set the oven at 180°C/350°F/gas 4. Combine the cheese, eggs and milk in a bowl. Add the breadcrumbs, with a little salt, if required. Mix thoroughly, then pour into the dish. Bake for 25-30 minutes, until set in the centre and browned on top.

SERVES 4

Curry Cheese Topper

The food values are for the cheese mixture and do not include the bread.

FOOD VALUES	TOTAL	PER PORTION
Protein	32g	16g
Carbohydrate	51g	26g
Fat	39g	20g
Fibre	3g	2g
kcals	668	334

15 *ml/1 tbsp apricot or mango chutney*
100 *g/4 oz mature Cheddar cheese, grated*
5 *ml/1 tsp curry powder*

Chop any large chunks in the chutney. Pound the cheese, chutney and curry powder together in a small bowl. Place the mixture in a covered container in the refrigerator. To use the mixture, spread it on freshly toasted bread and grill for 3-4 minutes until browned. Alternatively, serve on plain crackers or crispbreads.

SERVES 2

Welsh Rarebit

This is a traditional, tasty dish for lunch or supper. If you make it frequently, it is a good idea to substitute a full-flavoured reduced-fat cheese for ordinary Cheddar, but there is no reason to do this if you are aware of moderating the other sources of fat in your diet.

FOOD VALUES	TOTAL	PER PORTION (6)
Protein	48g	8g
Carbohydrate	12g	2g
Fat	84g	14g
Fibre	–	–
kcals	996	166

25 g/1 oz butter
15 ml/1 tbsp plain flour
75 ml/5 tbsp milk or 30 ml/ 2 tbsp milk and 45 ml/ 3 tbsp ale or beer
5 ml/1 tsp French mustard
few drops of Worcestershire sauce
175 g/6 oz Cheddar cheese, grated
salt and pepper

Melt the butter in a saucepan, stir in the flour and cook over gentle heat for 2-3 minutes, stirring constantly. Do not let the flour colour. Stir in the milk and blend to a smooth, thick mixture, then stir in the ale or beer, if used. Add the mustard and Worcestershire sauce.

Gradually add the cheese, stirring after each addition. Remove from the heat as soon as the mixture is smooth. Add salt and pepper to taste. Place in a covered container and chill when cool.

To use the rarebit, spread the mixture on freshly toasted bread and place under a preheated hot grill for 2-3 minutes until bubbling and lightly browned. Serve at once.

SERVES 4 TO 6

VARIATIONS

Buck Rarebit Make as for Welsh Rarebit, but top each slice with a poached egg.
Yorkshire Rarebit Make as for Welsh Rarebit, but add 4 grilled rindless back bacon rashers.

Irish Rarebit

FOOD VALUES	TOTAL	PER PORTION
Protein	34g	11g
Carbohydrate	38g	13g
Fat	59g	20g
Fibre	1g	–
kcals	803	268

100 g/4 oz mild Cheddar cheese, grated
60 ml/4 tbsp milk
25 g/1 oz butter
5 ml/1 tsp white wine vinegar
5 ml/1 tsp prepared English mustard
salt and pepper
10 ml/2 tsp chopped gherkin

Combine the cheese, milk and butter in a saucepan. Cook over gentle heat, stirring constantly, until the cheese has melted and the mixture is smooth and creamy. Stir in the vinegar and mustard, with salt and pepper to taste. Add the gherkin. Transfer to a container, cover and chill when cold.

To use the rarebit, spread the mixture on freshly toasted bread and grill briefly under moderate heat to brown the surface.

SERVES 3

NUTRITION NOTE

The food values are for the rarebit mixtures only and do not include the bread for either of the recipes given here. Use thick slices of wholemeal bread or a mixed grain loaf to provide some fibre and remember that there is no need to butter the toast as the fat content of the rarebit will moisten the toasted bread. Keep servings of rich snacks small and fill up on the bread, followed by fresh fruit or raw vegetable sticks.

NUTRITIOUS PACKED LUNCHES

If a packed lunch forms a regular part of the diet, then it is important that it makes a positive contribution rather than being dismissed as an aside to the main meals. If you have the time, make batches of home-baked quiches and large soda bread rolls to freeze ready for making up packed lunches. However, since most packed lunches are quickly assembled early in the morning it is a good idea to adopt a sound, practical approach which can always be varied when there is more time. Here are some reminders and ideas for every day.

SANDWICH MAKING

- Wholemeal bread has the advantage of providing fibre but it is a good idea to vary the types of bread which you use – include white, Granary, rye and wholemeal. Bread rolls, French bread and pita are also good alternatives for holding fillings. If you slice the bread yourself, cut it fairly thickly or buy medium or thick sliced bread. Although a thick sandwich may not look quite as elegant as a wafer-thin alternative, it is more satisfying and a better option in a balanced diet.
- It is a mistake to think that bread for sandwiches always has to be spread with butter or margarine. As long as the sandwich is neatly packed so that it does not fall apart, there is no need to spread any fat on the bread.
- Include salad vegetables: cucumber, lettuce, spring onions, tomatoes, grated carrot and sliced celery.
- Vary the sources of protein to avoid using high-fat fillings every day. Cheddar cheese is a great standby but try to include other foods, such as tuna (canned in brine), cooked chicken or turkey, lean cooked ham, low-fat soft cheese or crisply grilled and well-drained bacon.
- Sandwiches thinly spread with butter or margarine and yeast extract, then packed with lettuce and cucumber are delicious and nutritious.
- Fresh parsley makes a tasty sandwich filling: simply break off the stalks.
- Chutneys, pickles and relishes pep up simple sandwiches.

AVOIDING FATTY OR SUGARY SNACKS

Do not include packets of crips or other snacks in a lunch box – they contribute little food value and increase the fat content of the diet. Similarly, do not pack very sweet biscuits, sugary purchased cakes, confectionery or chocolate bars of any type. Plain biscuits or home-baked items are ideal occasional treats but they should not be an everyday item in the lunch box. The advantage of home-baked goods is that you control the sugar content which can be extremely high

(as can the fat level) in comparable bought items. It is also worth being aware of the added sugar in some cartons of fromage frais and yogurt – just because plain yogurt and low-fat fromage frais are recommended for frequent eating in a healthy diet it does not mean that all products based on these foods are the same. Always check the label.

USEFUL EXTRAS

- Pieces of celery, carrot, radish, chicory and mange tout are good to munch with sandwiches or with a small pot of light home-made dip, such as yogurt, low-fat soft cheese and chives.
- Always include fresh fruit in a lunch box. Apples, bananas and pears (not too ripe or they may be squashed) are extremely practical. Satsumas, oranges, peaches and nectarines or other juicy fruit, such as plums can be rather messy but older children and adults should be able to cope. A fresh fruit salad, packed in a sealed container, is also practical. Plums, melon, orange, grapefruit, grapes and mango may be included but avoid apples and bananas which discolour quickly.
- Lightly sweetened medium or low-fat fruit yogurts or pots of fromage frais satisfy a sweet tooth without adding excessive amounts of sugar.

BAKED GOODS

- Biscuits that are neither sugary nor too rich, such as digestive or rich tea, are a good regular choice.
- Teabreads tend to be lightly sweetened, which makes them a good option. They can be batch baked, then sliced before freezing ready for adding to the lunch box while frozen. Spread them thinly with butter, margarine or low-fat spread if necessary. Oatmeal Gingerbread (page 148) and Lunch Cake (page 150) are ideal.
- Small cakes or slices of large plain cake are a good occasional treat but avoid eating cake every day.

DRINKS

Sweetened drinks and full-strength fruit juices should not be consumed in large quantities, particularly by children, as they promote tooth decay. Mineral water and sugar-free drinks are the better option. Semi-skimmed or skimmed milk may be flavoured to make tempting and nutritious drinks. Alternatively, plain yogurt may be combined with fruit juice to make a refreshing drink.

For cold winter days, there is a wide choice of instant soup mixes, many of which are quite acceptable. However, nothing beats a flask of home-made soup. Chunky soups are difficult to pour and drink but puréed soups are satisfying, delicious and highly nutritious.

Omelette

The secret of a light omelette is to add water, not milk, to the mixture, beating it only sufficiently to mix the yolks and whites. The mixture must be cooked quickly until evenly and lightly set, then served when still moist. Have everything ready before you start to cook, including the diner, so that the omelette can be taken to the table as soon as it is ready.

FOOD VALUES	PER PORTION
Protein	15g
Carbohydrate	–
Fat	25g
Fibre	–
kcals	287

2 eggs
salt and pepper
15 ml/1 tbsp unsalted butter or margarine

Break the eggs into a bowl, add 15 ml/1 tbsp cold water, salt and pepper. Beat lightly with a fork. Thoroughly heat a frying pan or omelette pan. When it is hot, add the butter or margarine, tilting the pan so that the whole surface is lightly greased. Without drawing the pan off the heat, add the egg mixture. Leave to stand for 10 seconds.

Using a spatula, gently draw the egg mixture from the sides to the centre as it sets, allowing the uncooked egg mixture to run in to fill the gap. Do not stir or the mixture will scramble.

When the omelette is golden and set underneath, but still slightly moist on top, remove it from the heat. Loosen the edges by shaking the pan, using a round-bladed knife or the edge of a spatula, then flip one-third of the omelette towards the centre. Flip the opposite third over towards the centre. Tip the omelette on to a hot plate, folded sides underneath. Alternatively, the cooked omelette may be rolled out of the pan after the first folding, so that it is served folded in three. A simpler method is to fold the omelette in half in the pan, then slide it out on to the plate.

SERVES 1

OMELETTE FILLINGS

Fines Herbes Add 2.5 ml/½ tsp chopped fresh tarragon, 2.5 ml/½ tsp chopped fresh chervil, 5 ml/1 tsp chopped parsley and a few snipped chives to the beaten eggs. Food values as for main recipe.

Cheese Sprinkle 25 g/1 oz grated Cheddar over half the omelette before folding it.

FOOD VALUES	PER PORTION
Protein	29g
Carbohydrate	–
Fat	44g
Fibre	–
kcals	514

Ham Add 50 g/2 oz chopped ham to the egg mixture.

FOOD VALUES	PER PORTION
Protein	24g
Carbohydrate	–
Fat	28g
Fibre	–
kcals	347

Fish Add 50 g/2 oz flaked cooked white fish to the omelette just before folding.

FOOD VALUES	PER PORTION
Protein	26g
Carbohydrate	–
Fat	26g
Fibre	–
kcals	334

MRS BEETON'S TIP

In Mrs Beeton's day, most households would have a special omelette pan. When new, this would be seasoned by melting a little butter in the pan, sprinkling it with salt, and rubbing vigorously with a soft cloth. This process helped to prevent the egg mixture from sticking. The omelette pan would not be washed after use; instead it would be rubbed all over with a soft cloth. Salt would be used, if necessary, to remove any egg still sticking to the pan.

OMELETTE FILLINGS
continued

Bacon Grill 2 rindless bacon rashers until crisp; crumble into the centre of the omelette just before folding.

FOOD VALUES	PER PORTION
Protein	28g
Carbohydrate	–
Fat	43g
Fibre	–
kcals	495

Mushroom Thinly slice 50 g/2 oz mushrooms and quickly cook them in the minimum of butter or olive oil until very lightly cooked. Spoon into the centre of the omelette just before folding.

FOOD VALUES	PER PORTION
Protein	16g
Carbohydrate	–
Fat	32g
Fibre	1g
kcals	350

Shrimp or Prawn Add 50 g/2 oz shrimps or prawns and a squeeze of lemon juice to the omelette before folding.

FOOD VALUES	PER PORTION
Protein	26g
Carbohydrate	–
Fat	26g
Fibre	–
kcals	340

Chicken Chop 25 g/1 oz cooked chicken. Mix with 60 ml/4 tbsp simmering-hot white sauce or low-fat soft cheese. Spoon into the centre of the omelette before folding.

FOOD VALUES	PER PORTION
Protein	24g
Carbohydrate	7g
Fat	28g
Fibre	–
kcals	376

Breadcrumb Omelette

Some people find this more digestible than a conventional omelette as it is less rich. For a very light lunch, the omelette will serve two with a salad accompaniment.

FOOD VALUES	PER PORTION
Protein	40g
Carbohydrate	24g
Fat	61g
Fibre	–
kcals	798

25 g/1 oz fresh white breadcrumbs
250 ml/8 fl oz milk
4 eggs, separated
salt and pepper
20 ml/4 tsp butter

Put the breadcrumbs in a bowl, add the milk and leave to stand for 10 minutes. Stir in the egg yolks, with salt and pepper to taste. In a clean, dry bowl, whisk the egg whites until stiff; fold them into the breadcrumb mixture.

Place a frying pan or omelette pan over gentle heat. When it is hot, add the butter or margarine, tilting the pan so that the whole surface is lightly greased. Without drawing the pan off the heat, add the egg mixture; leave for 10 seconds. Preheat the grill.

Using a spatula, gently draw the egg mixture from the sides to the centre as it sets, allowing the uncooked egg mixture to run in to fill the gap. Do not stir or the mixture will scramble.

When the omelette is set and browned underneath, but still moist on top, remove it from the heat. Place under the hot grill for a few seconds to cook the top. Using a spatula, fold the omelette over in half and slide it out of the pan on to a heated plate.

SERVES 1

Spanish Omelette

Known as tortilla, a Spanish omelette is quite different from filled and folded omelettes or feather-light soufflé omelettes. It is a thick cake of potato and onion set in eggs, cut into wedges and served hot or cold. This classic potato omelette is quite delicious without any additional ingredients; however, the recipe is often varied to include red and green peppers or a mixture of vegetables, such as peas and green beans.

FOOD VALUES	TOTAL	PER PORTION (6)
Protein	60g	10g
Carbohydrate	133g	22g
Fat	80g	13g
Fibre	11g	2g
kcals	1456	243

675 g/1½ lb potatoes
225 g/8 oz onions, thinly sliced
salt and pepper
45 ml/3 tbsp olive oil
6 eggs, beaten

Cut the potatoes into 1 cm/½ inch cubes and mix them with the onions in a bowl. Add plenty of seasoning and mix well. Heat the oil in a heavy-bottomed frying pan which has fairly deep sides. Add the potatoes and onions, then cook, stirring and turning the vegetables often, until both potatoes and onions are tender. This takes about 25 minutes.

Pour the eggs over the potatoes and cook over medium heat, stirring, until the eggs begin to set. Press the vegetables down evenly and leave to set. Lower the heat to prevent the base of the omelette overbrowning before the eggs have set sufficiently.

Lay a large plate over the omelette and invert the pan to turn the omelette out on the plate. The base of the pan should be well greased but if it looks a little dry, add a little extra olive oil and heat it. Slide the omelette back into the pan and cook over medium to high heat for 3-5 minutes, until crisp and browned. Serve the omelette hot, warm or cold.

SERVES 4 TO 6

Scone Pizza

FOOD VALUES	TOTAL	PER PORTION (6)
Protein	109g	18g
Carbohydrate	167g	28g
Fat	88g	15g
Fibre	24g	4g
kcals	1855	309

fat for greasing
225 *g/8 oz self-raising wholemeal flour*
10 *ml/2 tsp baking powder*
salt and pepper
50 *g/2 oz margarine*
5 *ml/1 tsp dried marjoram*
2.5 *ml/½ tsp dried thyme*
150 *ml/¼ pint milk*

TOPPING
15 *ml/1 tbsp olive oil*
1 *onion, chopped*
1 *garlic clove (optional)*
15 *ml/1 tbsp roughly chopped capers*
30 *ml/2 tbsp chopped parsley*
1 (200 *g/7 oz) can tuna in brine, drained and flaked*
4 *large tomatoes, peeled and sliced*
100 *g/4 oz Cheddar cheese, grated*

Grease a large baking sheet. Set the oven at 220°C/425°F/gas 7. Mix the flour, baking powder and a little salt in a bowl, then rub in the margarine. Stir in the herbs and milk to make a soft dough. Knead the dough lightly.

Roll out the dough on a lightly floured surface into a 30 cm/12 inch circle. Lift the dough on to the prepared baking sheet and turn the edge over, pinching it neatly.

Heat the olive oil in a small saucepan. Add the onion and garlic (if used) and cook gently for about 10 minutes, until the onion is just beginning to soften. Off the heat, add the capers, parsley and flaked tuna. Spread this topping over the scone base, cover with tomato slices, then sprinkle with the cheese.

Bake for 20-25 minutes, until the topping is bubbling hot and golden and the base is risen, browned around the edges and cooked through. Serve cut into wedges.

SERVES 4 TO 6

Bean Salad with Tuna

FOOD VALUES	TOTAL	PER PORTION
Protein	112g	28g
Carbohydrate	159g	40g
Fat	63g	16g
Fibre	40g	10g
kcals	1608	402

450 g/1 lb dry flageolet beans, soaked overnight in water to cover
150 g/5 oz tomatoes, peeled, seeded and chopped
2 spring onions, finely chopped
1 (200 g/7 oz) can tuna in brine, drained and flaked

DRESSING
90 ml/6 tbsp olive oil or other salad oil
45 ml/3 tbsp white wine vinegar
1 garlic clove, crushed
15 ml/1 tbsp chopped parsley

Drain the beans and put them into a saucepan with fresh cold water to cover. Boil briskly for at least 10 minutes, then lower the heat and simmer for about 1 hour or until tender.

Meanwhile make the dressing by mixing all the ingredients in a screw-topped jar. Close the jar tightly; shake vigorously until well blended.

Drain the beans and put them in a bowl. Add the tomatoes, spring onions and tuna and mix well. Pour the cold dressing over the hot beans and the other ingredients and serve at once on warmed plates.

SERVES 4

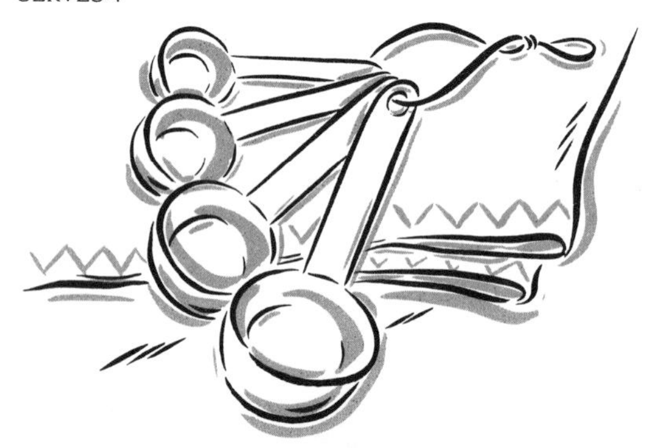

MRS BEETON'S TIP

A variety of beans may be combined with tuna: haricot, borlotti, butter and red kidney beans are all suitable. Remember that canned beans are excellent for speedy, highly successful salads.

Lentil and Onion Salad

FOOD VALUES	TOTAL	PER PORTION
Protein	37g	9g
Carbohydrate	76g	19g
Fat	43g	11g
Fibre	17g	4g
kcals	821	205

225 g/8 oz brown or green lentils
1 vegetable or onion stock cube
1 red onion, thinly sliced in rings
30 ml/2 tbsp finely chopped parsley

DRESSING
45 ml/3 tbsp light olive oil
salt and pepper
pinch of mustard powder
pinch of caster sugar
5 ml/1 tsp soy sauce
15 ml/1 tbsp red wine vinegar

Put the lentils in a saucepan with cold water to cover. Bring to the boil, add the crumbled stock cube, lower the heat and simmer for about 45 minutes until tender.

Meanwhile make the dressing by mixing all the ingredients in a screw-topped jar. Close the jar tightly and shake vigorously until well blended.

Drain the cooked lentils thoroughly, tip into a serving bowl and immediately add the dressing. Toss lightly, then add the onion rings with half the parsley. Allow the salad to stand for at least 1 hour before serving to allow the flavours to blend. Sprinkle with the remaining parsley.

SERVES 4

NUTRITION NOTE

Lentils and other pulses make satisfying, tasty salads which have a good 'bite' when properly prepared. They provide a useful supply of protein, making them ideal for main meals and for packing in sealed containers for packed lunches or picnics.

Pasta, Anchovy and Sweetcorn Salad

If you make salads of this type frequently, try one of the good-quality reduced-fat versions of mayonnaise or substitute a light fromage frais or plain yogurt.

FOOD VALUES	TOTAL	PER PORTION (4)
Protein	38g	9g
Carbohydrate	176g	44g
Fat	53g	13g
Fibre	8g	2g
kcals	1291	323

150 g/5 oz pasta shells
salt and pepper
60 ml/4 tbsp mayonnaise
1 (50 g/2 oz) can anchovies, drained and finely chopped
225 g/8 oz drained canned sweetcorn kernels
2 spring onions, finely chopped, to garnish

Cook the pasta in a large saucepan of boiling salted water for 10-12 minutes or until tender but still firm to the bite. Drain thoroughly. While still warm, stir in the mayonnaise. Set aside to cool.

Add the anchovies and sweetcorn, with salt and pepper to taste. Toss the salad lightly and garnish with the chopped spring onions.

SERVES 4 TO 6

MRS BEETON'S TIP

Use any decorative pasta for this dish. Spirals, bows or tiny cartwheels are all suitable. For a touch of colour, use tomato or spinach-flavoured pasta shapes.

Bean Sprout Salad

FOOD VALUES	TOTAL	PER PORTION
Protein	10g	2g
Carbohydrate	25g	6g
Fat	42g	11g
Fibre	7g	2g
kcals	510	128

225 g/8 oz bean sprouts
1 small orange, peeled and sliced
100 g/4 oz Chinese leaves, shredded
2 celery sticks, thinly sliced
1 small green pepper, seeded and cut into short, thin strips
salt and pepper

DRESSING
45 ml/3 tbsp olive oil or a mixture of olive and sunflower oil
15 ml/1 tbsp white wine vinegar
1 garlic clove, crushed
2.5 ml/½ tsp soy sauce
pinch of caster sugar

Pick over the bean sprouts, wash them well, then dry. Cut the orange slices into quarters.

Make the dressing by mixing all the ingredients in a screw-topped jar. Close the jar tightly and shake vigorously.

Combine the bean sprouts, Chinese leaves, celery, green pepper and orange in a bowl. Pour over the dressing and toss lightly. Season to taste and serve at once.

SERVES 4

NUTRITION NOTE

Fresh young bean sprouts are a good source of protein and uncooked green pepper is packed with vitamin C. To grow your own bean sprouts, place dried soya beans, mung beans or alfalfa seeds in a clean glass jar. The jar should be no more than one-sixth full. Cover the jar with a piece of muslin held in place by an elastic band. Fill the jar with cold water, then drain off the liquid. Store in a cool dark place. Rinse the beans in fresh water every day. They should start to sprout in 2-3 days and will be ready to eat in 5-6 days.

Waldorf Salad

FOOD VALUES	TOTAL	PER PORTION
Protein	6g	2g
Carbohydrate	56g	14g
Fat	56g	14g
Fibre	10g	3g
kcals	735	184

4 sharp red dessert apples
2 celery sticks, thinly sliced
25 g/1 oz chopped or broken walnuts
75 ml/5 tbsp mayonnaise
30 ml/2 tbsp lemon juice
pinch of salt
lettuce leaves (optional)

Core the apples, but do not peel them. Cut them into dice. Put them in a bowl with the celery and walnuts. Mix the mayonnaise with the lemon juice. Add salt to taste and fold into the apple mixture. Chill. Serve on a bed of lettuce leaves, if liked.

SERVES 4

VARIATION

Waldorf Salad with Chicken Make as above, but use only 2 apples. Add 350 g/12 oz diced cold cooked chicken. For extra flavour and colour, add 50 g/2 oz small seedless green grapes.

PUDDINGS AND DESSERTS

Baked Apples

FOOD VALUES	TOTAL	PER PORTION
Protein	4g	1g
Carbohydrate	168g	28g
Fat	1g	–
Fibre	13g	2g
kcals	663	111

6 cooking apples
75 g/3 oz sultanas, chopped
50 g/2 oz demerara sugar

Wash and core the apples. Cut around the skin of each apple with the tip of a sharp knife two-thirds of the way up from the base. Put the apples into an ovenproof dish, and fill the centres with the chopped sultanas.

Sprinkle the demerara sugar on top of the apples and pour 75 ml/5 tbsp water around them. Bake for 45-60 minutes, depending on the cooking quality and size of the apples.

Serve with a vanilla custard, fromage frais or plain yogurt.

SERVES 6

MICROWAVE TIP

Baked apples cook superbly in the microwave. Prepare as suggested above, but reduce the amount of water to 30 ml/2 tbsp. Cook for 10-12 minutes on High.

Brown Betty

FOOD VALUES	TOTAL	PER PORTION
Protein	24g	4g
Carbohydrate	338g	56g
Fat	7g	1g
Fibre	28g	5g
kcals	1418	236

at for greasing
kg/2¼ lb cooking apples
50 g/5 oz dried wholemeal breadcrumbs
rated rind and juice of 1 lemon
0 ml/4 tbsp golden syrup
00 g/4 oz demerara sugar

Grease a 1 litre/1¾ pint pie dish. Set the oven at 160°C/325°F/gas 3.

Peel and core the apples. Slice them thinly into a bowl. Coat the prepared pie dish with a thin layer of breadcrumbs, then fill with alternate layers of apples, lemon rind and breadcrumbs. Put the syrup, sugar and lemon juice into a saucepan. Add 30 ml/2 tbsp water. Heat until the syrup has dissolved, then pour the mixture over the layered pudding. Bake for 1-1¼ hours until the pudding is brown and the apple cooked. Serve with fromage frais, plain yogurt or a custard.

SERVES 6

MRS BEETON'S TIP

Use a tablespoon dipped in boiling water to measure the golden syrup. The syrup will slide off easily.

Baked Apples Stuffed with Rice and Nuts

FOOD VALUES	TOTAL	PER PORTION
Protein	19g	3g
Carbohydrate	195g	33g
Fat	39g	7g
Fibre	19g	3g
kcals	1150	192

6 medium cooking apples
25 g/1 oz flaked almonds or other nuts
40 g/1½ oz seedless raisins
25-50 g/1-2 oz boiled rice (preferably boiled in milk)
50 g/2 oz sugar or to taste
1 egg, beaten
30 ml/2 tbsp butter
raspberry or blackcurrant syrup to serve

Set the oven at 190°C/375°F/gas 5. Wash and core the apples but do not peel them. With a small rounded spoon, hollow out part of the flesh surrounding the core hole, taking care not to break the outside skin.

In a bowl, mix together the nuts, raisins and rice, using enough rice to make a stuffing for all the apples. Add the sugar, with enough egg to bind the mixture. Melt the butter and stir it into the mixture.

Fill the apples with the rice mixture. Place in a roasting tin and add hot water to a depth of 5 mm/¼ inch. Bake for 40 minutes or until the apples are tender. Remove the roasting tin from the oven and transfer the apples to a warmed serving platter, using a slotted spoon. Warm the fruit syrup and pour it over the apples.

SERVES 6

MICROWAVE TIP

The rice may be cooked in the microwave. Place 50 g/2 oz pudding rice in a large bowl with 30 ml/2 tbsp sugar. Stir in 600 ml/1 pint water, cover and cook on High for 2-5 minutes. Stir well, then stir in 300 ml/½ pint top-of-the-milk or reduced-fat single cream. Use 25-50 g/1-2 oz of the cooked rice for the above pudding and reserve the remainder.

Apple Crumble

FOOD VALUES	TOTAL	PER PORTION
Protein	16g	3g
Carbohydrate	361g	60g
Fat	64g	11g
Fibre	15g	3g
kcals	1992	332

fat for greasing
675 g/1½ lb cooking apples
100 g/4 oz granulated sugar
grated rind of 1 lemon
150 g/5 oz plain flour
50 g/2 oz butter or margarine
50 g/2 oz caster sugar
1.25 ml/¼ tsp ground ginger

Grease a 1 litre/1¾ pint pie dish. Set the oven at 180°C/350°F/gas 4.

Peel and core the apples. Slice them into a saucepan and add the granulated sugar and lemon rind. Stir in 50 ml/2 fl oz water, cover the pan and cook until the apples are soft. Spoon the apple mixture into the prepared dish and set aside.

Put the flour into a mixing bowl and rub in the butter or margarine until the mixture resembles fine breadcrumbs. Add the caster sugar and ginger and stir well. Sprinkle the mixture over the apples and press down lightly. Bake for 30-40 minutes until the crumble topping is golden brown.

SERVES 6

VARIATIONS

Instead of apples, use 675 g/1½ lb damsons, gooseberries, pears, plums, rhubarb or raspberries.

NUTRITION NOTE

Increase the fibre value of a fruit crumble by adding rolled oats to the topping. Reduce the flour to 100 g/4 oz and stir in 40 g/1½ oz rolled oats with the sugar and ginger – the resulting crumble has an excellent texture.

Traditional Apple Pie

FOOD VALUES	TOTAL	PER PORTION
Protein	35g	6g
Carbohydrate	439g	73g
Fat	148g	25g
Fibre	22g	4g
kcals	3117	520

675 g/1½ lb cooking apples
100 g/4 oz sugar
6 cloves
caster sugar for dredging

SHORT CRUST PASTRY
350 g/12 oz plain flour
4 ml/¾ tsp salt
175 g/6 oz margarine (or half butter, half lard)
flour for rolling out

Set the oven at 200°C/400°F/gas 6. To make the pastry, sift the flour and salt into a bowl, then rub in the margarine until the mixture resembles fine breadcrumbs. Add enough cold water to make a stiff dough. Press the dough together with your fingertips.

Roll out the pastry on a lightly floured surface and use just over half to line a 750 ml/1¼ pint pie dish. Peel, core and slice the apples. Place half in the pastry-lined dish, then add the sugar and cloves. Pile the remaining apples on top, cover with the remaining pastry and seal the edges. Brush the pastry with cold water and dredge with caster sugar.

Bake for 20 minutes, then lower the oven temperature to 180°C/350°F/gas 4 and bake for 20 minutes more. The pastry should be golden brown. Dredge with more caster sugar. Serve hot or cold.

SERVES 6

FREEZER TIP

The pie may be frozen cooked or uncooked. If cooked, cool completely, wrap in foil and overwrap in a polythene bag. Wrap an uncooked pie in the same way. Reheat or cook the unwrapped pie from frozen. A cooked pie will require 20 minutes at 200°C/400°F/gas 6, followed by 15-20 minutes at 180°C/350°F/gas 4. For an uncooked pie, bake at 200°C/400°F/gas 6 for 30 minutes, then at 190°C/375°F/gas 5 for about a further 40 minutes. The exact timing will depend on the depth of the pie dish. Before transferring the pie from freezer to oven, make sure that the dish will withstand the sudden change in temperature.

VARIATIONS

Blackberry and Apple Pie Use half blackberries and half apples and replace the cloves with 2.5 ml/½ tsp grated lemon rind.

FOOD VALUES	TOTAL	PER PORTION
Protein	37g	6g
Carbohydrate	428g	71g
Fat	148g	25g
Fibre	27g	5g
kcals	3091	515

Damson Pie Use damsons instead of apples, increase the sugar to 150 g/5 oz and omit the cloves.

FOOD VALUES	TOTAL	PER PORTION
Protein	40g	7g
Carbohydrate	507g	85g
Fat	148g	25g
Fibre	33g	6g
kcals	3395	566

Redcurrant and Raspberry Pie This is a winning combination. Use 450 g/1 lb redcurrants and 225 g/8 oz raspberries instead of apples. Reduce the sugar to 30 ml/2 tbsp and omit the cloves.

FOOD VALUES	TOTAL	PER PORTION
Protein	40g	7g
Carbohydrate	356g	59g
Fat	148g	25g
Fibre	33g	6g
kcals	2827	471

Rhubarb Pie Use rhubarb cut into 2 cm/¾ inch lengths instead of apples. Increase the sugar to 150 g/5 oz.

FOOD VALUES	TOTAL	PER PORTION
Protein	39g	7g
Carbohydrate	437g	76g
Fat	148g	25g
Fibre	20g	3g
kcals	3125	521

Jam Tart

FOOD VALUES	TOTAL	PER PORTION
Protein	15g	3g
Carbohydrate	169g	28g
Fat	55g	9g
Fibre	5g	1g
kcals	1188	198

60-90 *ml/4-6 tbsp firm jam*
beaten egg for glazing

SHORT CRUST PASTRY
150 *g/5 oz plain flour*
2.5 *ml/½ tsp salt*
65 *g/2½ oz margarine (or half butter, half lard)*
flour for rolling out

Set the oven at 200°C/400°F/gas 6. To make the pastry, sift the flour and salt into a bowl, then rub in the margarine until the mixture resembles fine breadcrumbs. Add enough cold water to make a stiff dough. Press the dough together lightly.

Roll out the pastry on a lightly floured surface and use to line a 20 cm/8 inch pie plate. Decorate the edge with any trimmings. Fill with jam and glaze the uncovered pastry with beaten egg.

Bake for 15 minutes or until the pastry is cooked. Serve hot or cold.

SERVES 6

NUTRITION NOTE

It is easy to dismiss many traditional puddings as 'unhealthy' without evaluating them. For example, a simple jam tart made with plain short crust pastry is not over-rich and the comparatively small amount of jam in a single slice does not make individual servings too sugary. Larger supermarkets and wholefood shops sell a wide variety of low-sugar jams – a good buy if you do eat quite a lot of sweet preserves.

Banana Flan

FOOD VALUES	TOTAL	PER PORTION
Protein	33g	6g
Carbohydrate	281g	47g
Fat	62g	10g
Fibre	8g	1g
kcals	1748	291

1 whole egg, separated, plus 1 yolk
50 *g/2 oz caster sugar*
30 *ml/2 tbsp plain flour*
30 *ml/2 tbsp cornflour*
300 *ml/½ pint milk*
2.5 *ml/½ tsp vanilla essence*
3 *bananas*
30 *ml/2 tbsp warmed and sieved apricot jam*

SHORT CRUST PASTRY
100 *g/4 oz plain flour*
1.25 *ml/¼ tsp salt*
50 *g/2 oz margarine (or half butter, half lard)*
flour for rolling out

Set the oven at 200°C/400°F/gas 6. To make the pastry, sift the flour and salt into a bowl, then rub in the margarine. Add enough cold water to make a stiff dough. Press the dough together with your fingers.

Roll out the pastry on a lightly floured surface and use to line a 20 cm/8 inch flan tin or ring placed on a baking sheet. Line the pastry with greaseproof paper and fill with baking beans. Bake blind for 20 minutes, then remove the paper and beans. Return to the oven for 5-7 minutes, then cool completely.

Make the filling. In a bowl, mix both egg yolks with the sugar. Beat until thick and pale in colour, then beat in the flours. Add enough of the milk to make a smooth paste. Pour the rest of the milk into a saucepan and bring to just below boiling point. Pour on to the yolk mixture, stirring constantly, then return the mixture to the pan. Cook over low heat, stirring, until the mixture boils and thickens. Remove from the heat.

Whisk the egg white in a clean, grease-free bowl until stiff. Fold it into the custard with the vanilla essence. Return to the heat and cook for a couple of minutes, then cool. Cover the surface of the custard with dampened greaseproof paper while cooling.

Spoon the cold custard into the flan case and top with sliced bananas. Glaze immediately with hot apricot jam and leave to set. Serve the flan cold.

SERVES 6

Banana Bonanza

FOOD VALUES	TOTAL	PER PORTION
Protein	15g	4g
Carbohydrate	105g	26g
Fat	1g	–
Fibre	3g	1g
kcals	466	117

4 bananas (about 450 g/ 1 lb)
15 ml/1 tbsp lemon juice
30 ml/2 tbsp soft dark brown sugar
250 ml/8 fl oz fromage frais

Mash the bananas with the lemon juice in a bowl. Stir in the sugar and fromage frais. Serve at once.

SERVES 4

Banana Snow

FOOD VALUES	TOTAL	PER PORTION
Protein	44g	7g
Carbohydrate	189g	32g
Fat	18g	3g
Fibre	7g	1g
kcals	1043	174

6 bananas (about 675 g/ 1½ lb)
50 g/2 oz sugar
15 ml/1 tbsp lemon juice
125 ml/4 fl oz double cream
300 ml/½ pint plain yogurt
3 egg whites
25 g/1 oz flaked almonds, toasted

Mash the bananas in a bowl with the sugar and lemon juice, or purée in a blender or food processor. Tip into a bowl. Whip the cream in a bowl until it just holds its shape, then fold it into the banana purée with the yogurt.

In a clean, grease-free bowl, whisk the egg whites until they form stiff peaks, then fold into the banana mixture. Pile into one large or six dishes. Sprinkle with the almonds.

SERVES 6

Quick Batter Puddings

Serve poached fruit, such as plums, cherries or apricots, with these puffy puddings.

FOOD VALUES	TOTAL	PER PORTION
Protein	17g	4g
Carbohydrate	72g	18g
Fat	33g	8g
Fibre	2g	1g
kcals	640	160

25 g/1 oz butter plus extra for greasing
150 ml/¼ pint milk
50 g/2 oz plain flour
25 g/1 oz caster sugar
grated rind of 1 lemon
1 egg

Set the oven at 220°C/425°F/gas 7. Butter four ramekin dishes or small baking dishes and place them on a baking sheet.

Heat the butter and milk in a small saucepan until the butter has melted; cool. Mix the flour, sugar and lemon rind in a bowl, then make a well in the centre and add the egg. Add a little milk and beat the egg with a little of the flour mixture. Work in the flour, adding a little more milk, to make a thick batter. Beat until smooth. Gradually beat in the rest of the milk.

Divide the batter between the dishes and bake for 20–30 minutes, until the puddings are risen, golden and set. Serve at once.

SERVES 4

Apple Batter Pudding

An old favourite which can be varied by using different fruit, both fresh and dried. Alternative fresh fruit include cherries, plums, gooseberries and thickly sliced rhubarb. Remove the stones from fruit before using them in the pudding.

FOOD VALUES	TOTAL	PER PORTION
Protein	26g	7g
Carbohydrate	182g	46g
Fat	30g	8g
Fibre	10g	3g
kcals	1059	265

25 g/1 *oz cooking fat*
450 *g*/1 *lb cooking apples*
50 *g/2 oz sugar*
grated rind of ½ lemon

BATTER
100 *g/4 oz plain flour*
1.25 *ml/¼ tsp salt*
1 *egg, beaten*
250 *ml/8 fl oz milk, or half milk and half water*

Make the batter. Sift the flour and salt into a bowl, make a well in the centre and add the beaten egg. Stir in half the milk (or all the milk, if using a mixture of milk and water), gradually working in the flour. Beat vigorously until the mixture is smooth and bubbly, then stir in the rest of the milk (or the water).

Set the oven at 220°C/425°F/gas 7. Put the fat into a 28 × 18 cm/11 × 7 inch baking tin and heat in the oven for 5 minutes.

Meanwhile peel, core and thinly slice the apples. Remove the baking tin from the oven and swiftly arrange the apples on the base. Sprinkle with the sugar and lemon rind. Pour the batter over the top and bake for 30-35 minutes until brown and risen. Cut into 4 pieces and serve at once, with a little clear honey if liked.

SERVES 4

VARIATIONS

Apricot Batter Pudding Put 100 g/4 oz dried apricots in a bowl and add just enough water to cover. Soak until soft, preferably overnight. Transfer the apricots and soaking liquid to a pan and simmer for 15 minutes. Drain. Make the batter as described in the main recipe, heat the fat, and layer the apricots on the base of the baking tin. Proceed as in the main recipe.

FOOD VALUES	TOTAL	PER PORTION
Protein	29g	7g
Carbohydrate	179g	45g
Fat	30g	8g
Fibre	9g	2g
kcals	1060	265

Dried Fruit Batter Pudding Make the batter and heat the fat as in the main recipe, then spread 50 g/ 2 oz mixed dried fruit over the base of the tin. Sprinkle with 2.5 ml/½ tsp mixed spice or cinnamon. Proceed as in the main recipe.

FOOD VALUES	TOTAL	PER PORTION
Protein	26g	7g
Carbohydrate	176g	44g
Fat	30g	8g
Fibre	4g	1g
kcals	1036	259

Black Cap Puddings Make the batter as in the main recipe. Grease 12 deep patty tins and divide 50 g/2 oz currants between them. Pour in enough batter to half fill each tin and bake for 15-20 minutes. Turn out to serve. Food values as above, allowing three puddings per portion.

DESSERTS IN A BALANCED DIET

Although it is not a good idea to serve a sweet, rich pudding every day, there is absolutely no reason to ban traditional desserts. It is, however, important to take into account any puddings which are included in everyday meals. For example, if you have a fruit pie for dessert, it is a good idea to balance this by serving other dishes which are quite low in fat to compensate for the rich pastry. This must be considered along with the other foods eaten and, of course, the individual portion sizes. Include fresh fruit or lightly sweetened low-fat desserts on the majority of occasions.

THE FOOD VALUE OF DESSERTS

Milk puddings and custards are two examples of desserts which are usually lightly sweetened and which make a valuable contribution to the overall food value of the diet. Young children will benefit from desserts made with whole milk; there is no reason to avoid whole milk on principle if the overall fat content of the diet is moderated. However, these puddings can be made using semi-skimmed or skimmed milk if necessary.

Fresh fruit salads (unsweetened) make a useful contribution to the vitamin content of the diet and may be served with plain low-fat yogurt or fromage frais.

Cream, Custard and Sauces

Sensible-sized portions of comparatively plain desserts or puddings which may be only moderately sweet or rich are often rendered less suitable for everyday consumption by the addition of large quantities of cream, creamy custard or syrupy sauces. The obvious solution – substituting yogurt or fromage frais – is not necessarily the best option in terms of healthy eating. Some types of full-fat yogurt are themselves extremely rich as, indeed, is full-fat fromage frais – in many cases you may as well dollop on the double cream and at least recognize the dessert for what it is. So, when a recipe suggests serving yogurt or fromage frais as an accompaniment, be sure to select low-fat varieties.

Fruit purées, which may be lightly sweetened if necessary, are good replacements for heavy syrups and very sweet sauces. Raspberries, strawberries and cooked apples purée well. Bananas may be mashed with yogurt to make a creamy dessert topping.

SIMPLE FRUIT SALADS

Fruit is definitely the healthiest choice of dessert – an apple, orange, banana or other piece of fruit will satisfy the taste for pudding without the need for any additional sweetening or rich topping. The wide variety of exotic fruit which is

now available has made the old-fashioned fruit salad a thing of the past and, sadly, transformed an inexpensive everyday dessert into a special dish. For healthy everyday sweets, rely on inexpensive favourites but dispense with the classic quantity of sugar syrup which is unnecessary if the right choice of fruit is made.

- Squeeze the juice from an orange and sweeten it very lightly with a little honey then use this as a dressing for fruits which discolour, such as apples or bananas.
- Quarter, core and slice apples across into neat pieces, then toss them in the orange juice mixture to prevent them from discolouring. Top with chopped dates and toasted hazelnuts.
- Select bananas which are just ripe, not too soft, then slice them thinly. Arrange in a dish with sliced, peeled kiwi fruit and serve with fromage frais or plain low-fat yogurt.
- Whole seedless grapes simply need rinsing and drying on absorbent kitchen paper before tossing into a salad. They are good with orange segments and chopped ready-to-eat dried apricots.
- To quickly prepare citrus fruit for an everyday salad, cut off all peel and pith from outside, then halve and slice the fruit, removing all pips and pith from the middle. Do this on a large plate to catch juices.

Interesting Extras

Make a simple combination of fruit more exciting by adding a few chopped walnuts, almonds or unsalted cashew nuts. Simmer or soak a few raisins or sultanas in orange or apple juice to plump them up, then add them to the salad. Roast a few sunflower seeds in a small, heavy-bottomed saucepan and allow to cool before sprinkling over the salad. Chop ready-to-eat dried apricots or peaches and add these to the salad.

Fruit Salad Jellies

Set fruit in jelly made from fruit juice and gelatine or a bought, low-sugar jelly. Place the prepared fruit in individual dishes and pour in jelly to cover, then chill until set.

Seasonal Fruits

Take advantage of soft fruits in season – strawberries, raspberries, currants (red and black) and blackberries – to enliven simple fruit salads.

Poached Fruit

Detailed information on stewing fruit is included in the chapter on breakfast. Stewed or poached fruit is a popular choice for dessert and the only consideration to ensure it fits into a healthy eating plan is to avoid adding excessive amounts of sugar. Stewed fruit tends to be cooked for longer than poached fruit, which may be cut in larger portions or left whole and simmered very gently until only just tender.

- Poach fruit in unsweetened fruit juice instead of making a syrup. For example, apples and pears are delicious cooked in orange juice. Once the fruit is cooked, it may be transferred to a serving dish and the cooking liquid may be boiled until greatly reduced to serve as a glaze for the fruit.
- Combine tart and naturally sweet fruits – for example, sliced bananas go well with tart apples, rhubarb or plums. Add the bananas towards the end of cooking, so that they are heated rather than cooked.

Fruit Fools and Whips

Rhubarb, plums, blackberries, blackcurrants and gooseberries all make tangy fools. Poach and purée the fruit, then leave it to cool. Very sharp fruit, such as gooseberries or rhubarb, should be sweetened before cooking but it is best to allow other types to cool and to taste them before adding sugar.

Lightly sweetened custard may be used as a base and yogurt or fromage frais may be added for a creamy result. Fold the fruit purée into the custard mixture, spoon the fool into glass dishes and chill.

Quick whips and fools can be made by folding yogurt or fromage frais into fruit purée without any custard. To thicken thin purées blend a little arrowroot or cornflour with cold water and stir in some of the hot fruit, then stir the mixture into the remaining fruit purée. Thoroughly chilled unsweetened evaporated milk may be whipped to a thick foam and folded into chilled, thickened fruit purées before serving.

FRESH FRUIT IDEAS

- Grill bananas in their skins until black, then peel back the skin to serve.
- Layer prepared fresh fruit in a gratin dish and top with fromage frais or yogurt. Chill well, then top with a layer of brown sugar and place under a preheated grill until the sugar melts and caramelizes.
- Poach peeled pears in orange juice to make a delicious dessert. Add a little sugar, if liked, or sweetener to taste.
- Purée strawberries, raspberries or bananas and add them to a freshly cooked vanilla blancmange. Pour into serving glasses, cool and chill.

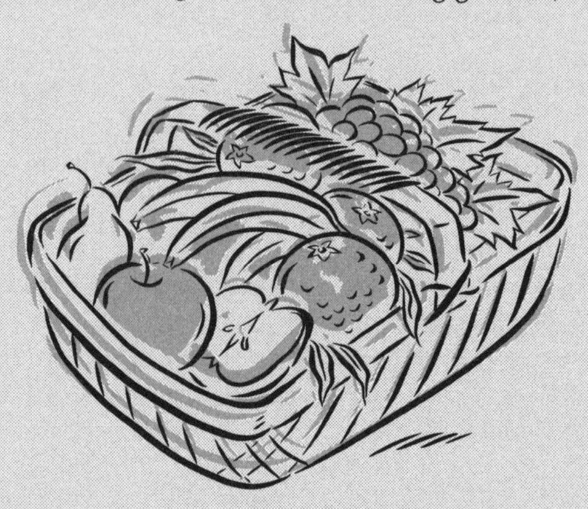

Chocolate Semolina

FOOD VALUES	TOTAL	PER PORTION (5)
Protein	36g	4g
Carbohydrate	190g	38g
Fat	54g	11g
Fibre	–	–
kcals	1346	269

800 ml/27 fl oz milk
65 g/2½ oz semolina
75 g/3 oz plain chocolate
50 g/2 oz caster sugar
few drops of vanilla essence

Heat 750 ml/1¼ pints of the milk in a heavy-bottomed saucepan. Sprinkle in the semolina, stir well, and simmer for 15-20 minutes or until the semolina is cooked.

Meanwhile, grate the chocolate into a second pan, add the remaining milk and heat until the chocolate has melted. Stir into the semolina with the sugar and essence, and serve at once.

SERVES 4 TO 5

MRS BEETON'S TIP

Chocolate semolina is also delicious chilled. Follow the recipe, then turn the semolina into a suitable, heatproof, serving dish. Cover the surface of the semolina with dampened greaseproof paper, pressing it on to prevent a skin forming as the dessert cools. When cold, place in the refrigerator for several hours before serving. Top with sliced bananas and fresh orange segments, if liked.

Baked Custard

Egg dishes should be cooked by gentle heat. If the custard is allowed to boil, the protein will no longer be able to hold moisture in suspension and the resultant pudding will be watery. It is therefore a wise precaution to use a bain marie or water bath.

FOOD VALUES	TOTAL	PER PORTION
Protein	39g	10g
Carbohydrate	50g	13g
Fat	39g	10g
Fibre	–	–
kcals	693	173

fat for greasing
500 *ml*/17 *fl oz milk*
3 *eggs*
25 *g*/1 *oz caster sugar*
grated nutmeg

Grease a baking dish. Set the oven at 150°C/300°F/gas 2. In a saucepan, bring the milk to just below boiling point. Put the eggs and sugar into a bowl, mix well, then stir in the scalded milk. Strain the custard mixture into the prepared dish. Sprinkle the nutmeg on top.

Stand the dish in a roasting tin and add enough hot water to come halfway up the sides of the dish. Bake for 1 hour or until the custard is set in the centre.

SERVES 4

NUTRITION NOTE

Baked custard makes a significant protein contribution to the meal – the ideal pudding to follow a vegetable dish or salad which may not include a good quantity of high-quality protein. Custards are also ideal for young children who may be going through difficult eating phases, when you may be concerned about the overall value of the amount of food they eat for their main meal.

Banana Custard

FOOD VALUES	TOTAL	PER PORTION
Protein	38g	10g
Carbohydrate	87g	22g
Fat	31g	8g
Fibre	3g	1g
kcals	758	190

500 *ml*/17 *fl oz milk*
3 *eggs plus* 2 *yolks*
25 *g*/1 *oz caster sugar*
few drops of vanilla essence
3 *bananas* (*about* 400 *g*/ 14 *oz*)
toasted flaked almonds to decorate

In a saucepan, bring the milk to just below boiling point. Put the eggs and sugar into a bowl, mix well, then stir in the scalded milk and vanilla essence. Strain the custard mixture into a heavy-bottomed saucepan or a heatproof bowl placed over a saucepan of simmering water. Alternatively, use a double saucepan, but make sure the water does not touch the upper pan.

Cook the custard over very gentle heat for 15-25 minutes, stirring all the time with a wooden spoon, until the custard thickens to the consistency of single cream. Stir well around the sides as well as the base of the pan or bowl to prevent the formation of lumps, especially if using a double saucepan. Do not let the custard boil or it may curdle. As soon as the custard thickens, pour it into a jug to stop further cooking. Peel and slice the bananas and stir them into the custard. Stand the jug in a bowl of hot water for 5 minutes to allow the flavours to blend. Spoon into a serving dish or individual dishes and decorate with flaked almonds.

If the custard is to be served cold, pour it into a bowl and cover the surface with a piece of dampened greaseproof paper to prevent discoloration and a skin forming. When cold, pour into a serving dish and decorate as desired.

SERVES 4

Bread and Butter Pudding

When the weather is dull and dreary, lift the spirits with this comforting old favourite.

FOOD VALUES	TOTAL	PER PORTION
Protein	38g	10g
Carbohydrate	129g	32g
Fat	51g	13g
Fibre	3g	1g
kcals	1096	274

butter for greasing
4 *thin slices of bread (about* 100 *g*/4 *oz)*
25 *g*/1 *oz butter*
50 *g*/2 *oz sultanas or currants*
pinch of ground nutmeg or cinnamon
400 *ml*/14 *fl oz milk*
2 *eggs*
25 *g*/1 *oz granulated sugar*

Grease a 1 litre/1¾ pint pie dish. Cut the crusts off the bread and spread the slices with the butter. Cut the bread into squares or triangles and arrange in alternate layers, buttered side up, in the dish with the sultanas or currants. Sprinkle each layer lightly with nutmeg or cinnamon. Arrange the top layer of bread in an attractive pattern.

Warm the milk in a saucepan to about 65°C/150°F. Do not let it approach boiling point. Put the eggs in a bowl. Add most of the sugar. Beat with a fork and stir in the milk. Strain the custard mixture over the bread, sprinkle some nutmeg and the remaining sugar on top, and leave to stand for 30 minutes. Set the oven at 180°C/350°F/gas 4.

Bake for 30-40 minutes until the custard is set and the top is lightly browned.

SERVES 4

PRESSURE COOKER TIP

Use a dish that fits in the pressure cooker. Cover the pudding with foil or greased greaseproof paper, tied down securely. Cook at 15lb pressure for 9 minutes. Reduce pressure slowly, then brown the pudding under the grill.

Rice Pudding

This basic recipe works equally well with flaked rice, sago or flaked tapioca.

FOOD VALUES	TOTAL	PER PORTION (4)
Protein	39g	10g
Carbohydrate	213g	53g
Fat	55g	14g
Fibre	–	–
kcals	1449	362

butter for greasing
100 *g/4 oz pudding rice*
1 *litre/1¾ pints milk*
pinch of salt
50-75 *g/2-3 oz caster sugar*
15 *g/½ oz butter (optional)*
1.25 *ml/¼ tsp grated nutmeg*

Butter a 1.75 litre/3 pint pie dish. Wash the rice in cold water, drain and put it into the dish with the milk. Leave to stand for 30 minutes.

Set the oven at 150°C/300°F/gas 2. Stir the salt and sugar into the milk mixture and sprinkle with flakes of butter, if used, and nutmeg.

Bake for 2-2½ hours or until the pudding is thick and creamy, and brown on the top. The pudding is better if it cooks even more slowly, at 120°C/250°F/gas ½ for 4-5 hours.

SERVES 4 TO 5

PRESSURE COOKER TIP

Bring all the ingredients to the boil in the open cooker, stirring. Reduce the heat so that the milk just bubbles. Put the lid on and bring to 15 lb pressure without increasing the heat. Cook for 12 minutes. Reduce pressure slowly.

Windsor Pudding

FOOD VALUES	TOTAL	PER PORTION
Protein	28g	5g
Carbohydrate	195g	33g
Fat	18g	3g
Fibre	8g	1g
kcals	1003	167

butter for greasing
40 *g*/1½ *oz long-grain rice*
350 *ml*/12 *fl oz milk*
450 *g*/1 *lb cooking apples*
grated rind of ½ lemon
50 *g*/2 *oz caster sugar*
3 *egg whites*

Butter a 1 litre/1¾ pint pudding basin or soufflé dish. Wash the rice, drain thoroughly and place in a saucepan with the milk. Simmer for 45-60 minutes or until the rice is tender and all the milk has been absorbed. Cool slightly. Peel, core and roughly chop the apples. Stew in a covered, heavy-bottomed saucepan until soft. Shake the pan from time to time to prevent the apples from sticking. Prepare a steamer or half fill a large saucepan with water. Bring to the boil.

Purée the apples with the lemon rind in a blender or food processor. Alternatively, rub the apples through a sieve into a bowl, in which case add the grated lemon rind afterwards. Stir in the cooked rice and sugar.

In a clean, grease-free bowl, whisk the egg whites until fairly stiff and stir them into the apple mixture. Spoon the mixture into the prepared pudding basin or soufflé dish, cover with greased greaseproof paper or foil and secure with string.

Put the pudding in the perforated part of the steamer, or stand it on an old saucer or plate in the pan of boiling water. The water should come halfway up the sides of the basin. Cover the pan tightly and steam the pudding over gently simmering water for 45 minutes. Serve hot.

SERVES 6

MRS BEETON'S TIP

Windsor pudding is very light and it can be difficult to turn out. Placing a small circle of non-stick baking parchment in the bottom of the basin helps. Alternatively, serve the pudding straight from the basin or dish.

Lemon Rice

A meringue topping gives this simple pudding a touch of class.

FOOD VALUES	TOTAL	PER PORTION
Protein	35g	6g
Carbohydrate	226g	38g
Fat	34g	6g
Fibre	–	–
kcals	1297	216

butter for greasing
50 g/2 oz long-grain rice
500 ml/17 fl oz milk
pinch of salt
pared rind and juice of 1 lemon
75 g/3 oz granulated sugar
2 eggs, separated
45 ml/3 tbsp smooth seedless jam
50 g/2 oz caster sugar, plus extra for dredging

Butter a 1 litre/1¾ pint pie dish. Set the oven at 160°C/325°F/gas 3. Wash the rice and put it in a double saucepan with the milk, salt and lemon rind; simmer for about 1 hour or until tender. Remove the rind and stir in the granulated sugar. Cool slightly.

Stir the egg yolks and lemon juice into the rice. Pour into the pie dish and bake for 20-25 minutes. Lower the oven temperature to 140°C/275°F/gas 1.

Spread the jam on top of the pudding. In a clean, grease-free bowl, whisk the egg whites until stiff, and fold in the caster sugar. Pile on top of the pudding, dredge with a little extra caster sugar, and return to the oven. Bake for 20-30 minutes until the meringue is set and coloured.

SERVES 6

Blancmange Mould

Blancmange may be made using ground rice or arrowroot instead of the cornflour given below. The quantities will be the same. Traditionally, blancmange was a white mould which was flavoured with sweet and bitter almonds. Use natural almond essence to give this mould the best flavour.

FOOD VALUES	TOTAL	PER PORTION
Protein	32g	5g
Carbohydrate	170g	28g
Fat	40g	7g
Fibre	–	–
kcals	1123	187

75 g/3 oz cornflour
1 litre/1¾ pints milk
50 g/2 oz sugar
a little almond essence

In a bowl, blend the cornflour to a smooth paste with a little of the cold milk. Bring the remaining milk to the boil in a saucepan.

Pour the boiling milk on to the cornflour mixture, stirring all the time. Pour the mixture back into the pan and heat gently, stirring all the time until the mixture simmers and thickens. Allow to simmer for 5-10 minutes, stirring occasionally.

Remove the pan from the heat and stir in the sugar. Add almond essence to taste, stir well, then pour the blancmange into a wetted 1.1 litre/2 pint mould. Press dampened greaseproof paper or microwave cooking film on to the surface of the blancmange and cool.

Chill the cooled blancmange for at least 2 hours, or until set. Unmould the blancmange just before serving.

SERVES 6

MRS BEETON'S TIP

If arrowroot is used instead of cornflour, the pan should be removed from the heat as soon as the mixture has reached a full boil. If arrowroot is cooked for any length of time after boiling, it tends to thin down.

FLAVOURINGS

To keep the mould a creamy colour, vanilla or grated lemon rind may be added instead of the almond essence. However, the mixture may also be flavoured with ingredients that add colour although the result is not strictly a blancmange.

Chocolate Either add 30 ml/2 tbsp cocoa to the cornflour and mix it to a paste or add 175 g/6 oz plain chocolate, broken into squares, to the cooked mixture. Stir the mixture until the chocolate has melted before pouring it into the wetted mould. Food values are for plain chocolate.

FOOD VALUES	TOTAL	PER PORTION
Protein	41g	7g
Carbohydrate	283g	47g
Fat	91g	15g
Fibre	–	–
kcals	2041	340

Coffee Dissolve 15 ml/1 tbsp instant coffee in 15 ml/1 tbsp boiling water, then stir in 30 ml/2 tbsp rum. Stir this essence into the cooked mixture before pouring it into the mould.

FOOD VALUES	TOTAL	PER PORTION
Protein	33g	6g
Carbohydrate	170g	28g
Fat	40g	7g
Fibre	–	–
kcals	1195	199

Strawberry Substitute 300 ml/½ pint fresh strawberry purée for the same volume of milk, adding it to the cornflour mixture before stirring in the boiling milk.

FOOD VALUES	TOTAL	PER PORTION
Protein	26g	4g
Carbohydrate	182g	30g
Fat	28g	5g
Fibre	5g	1g
kcals	1046	174

Sweet Soufflé Omelette

FOOD VALUES	PER PORTION
Protein	15g
Carbohydrate	13g
Fat	25g
Fibre	–
kcals	334

2 eggs, separated
5 ml/1 tsp caster sugar
few drops of vanilla essence
15 ml/1 tbsp unsalted butter or margarine
icing sugar for dredging

In a large bowl, whisk the yolks until creamy. Add the sugar and vanilla essence with 30 ml/2 tbsp water, then whisk again. In a clean, grease-free bowl, whisk the egg whites until stiff. Place an 18 cm/7 inch omelette pan over gentle heat and when it is hot, add the butter or margarine. Tilt the pan to grease the whole of the inside. Pour out any excess. Fold the egg whites into the yolk mixture carefully until evenly distributed, using a metal spoon (see Mrs Beeton's Tip). Heat the grill to moderate.

Pour the egg mixture into the omelette pan, level the top very lightly, and cook for 1-2 minutes over moderate heat until the omelette is golden brown on the underside and moist on top. (Use a palette knife to lift the edge to look underneath.)

Put the pan under the grill for 5-6 minutes until the omelette is risen and lightly browned on the top. The texture of the omelette should be firm yet spongy. Remove from the heat as soon as it is ready, as over-cooking tends to make it tough. Run a palette knife gently round the edge and underneath to loosen it. Make a mark across the middle at right angles to the pan handle but do not cut the surface. Put the chosen filling on one half, raise the handle of the pan and double the omelette over. Turn gently on to a warm plate, dredge with icing sugar and serve at once.

SERVES 1

MRS BEETON'S TIP

When folding the beaten egg whites into the omelette mixture, be very careful not to overmix, as it is the air incorporated in the frothy whites that causes the omelette to rise.

FILLINGS

Cherry Omelette Stone 100 g/4 oz dark cherries, or use canned ones. Warm with 30 ml/2 tbsp cherry jam and 15 ml/1 tbsp kirsch. Spread over the omelette.

FOOD VALUES	PER PORTION
Protein	16g
Carbohydrate	45g
Fat	25g
Fibre	1g
kcals	494

Creamy Peach Omelette Stone and roughly chop 1 ripe peach, then mix it with 45 ml/3 tbsp cream cheese. Add a little icing sugar to taste and mix well until softened. Spread over the omelette.

FOOD VALUES	PER PORTION
Protein	17g
Carbohydrate	25g
Fat	44g
Fibre	2g
kcals	563

Jam Omelette Warm 45 ml/3 tbsp fruity jam and spread over the omelette.

FOOD VALUES	PER PORTION
Protein	15g
Carbohydrate	47g
Fat	25g
Fibre	–
kcals	465

Lemon Omelette Add the grated rind of ½ lemon to the egg yolk. Warm 45 ml/3 tbsp lemon curd with 10 ml/2 tsp lemon juice, and spread over the omelette.

FOOD VALUES	PER PORTION
Protein	15g
Carbohydrate	44g
Fat	28g
Fibre	–
kcals	476

Oatmeal Flummery

FOOD VALUES	TOTAL	PER PORTION (6)
Protein	17g	3g
Carbohydrate	114g	19g
Fat	14g	2g
Fibre	11g	2g
kcals	620	103

150 g/5 oz fine oatmeal
juice of 1 orange
15 ml/1 tbsp caster sugar or honey

Put the oatmeal in a large bowl. Add 500 ml/17 fl oz water and soak for 24 hours.

Transfer the oatmeal mixture to a large measuring jug. Measure an equal volume of water. Place the oatmeal mixture and measured water in a large bowl, and soak for a further 24 hours.

Strain the mixture through a fine sieve into a heavy-bottomed saucepan, squeezing or pressing the oatmeal to extract as much of the floury liquid as possible. Add the orange juice and sugar or honey. Stir over gentle heat for 15-30 minutes or until the mixture boils and is very thick. Serve warm.

SERVES 4 TO 6

TEA-TIME BAKING

Sweet Brown Scones

These scones are delicious filled with low-fat soft cheese or butter and spread with a little honey.

FOOD VALUES	TOTAL	PER PORTION (10)
Protein	40g	4g
Carbohydrate	234g	23g
Fat	55g	6g
Fibre	21g	2g
kcals	1528	153

fat for greasing
225 *g/8 oz wholemeal or brown flour*
2.5 *ml/½ tsp salt*
2.5 *ml/½ tsp baking powder*
50 *g/2 oz margarine*
50 *g/2 oz soft light brown sugar*
50 *g/2 oz seedless raisins*
1 *egg, plus milk to give* 125-150 *ml/4-5 fl oz*
flour for rolling out

Grease a baking sheet. Set the oven at 220°C/425°F/ gas 7. Mix the flour, salt and baking powder in a large bowl. Rub in the margarine, then stir in the sugar and dried fruit. Beat the egg and milk together. Reserve a little for brushing the tops of the scones and add the rest to the dry ingredients. Mix to a soft dough. Knead lightly.

Roll out the dough on a floured surface to just over 1 cm/½ inch thick. Cut into rounds, using a 6 cm/ 2½ inch cutter. Re-roll the trimmings and re-cut. Place the scones on the prepared baking sheet. Brush the tops with the reserved egg and milk mixture.

Bake for 10-15 minutes. Serve warm or cold, split and buttered.

MAKES 10 TO 12

VARIATION

Bran Scones Use 175 g/6 oz self-raising flour, 2.5 ml/½ tsp salt, 5 ml/1 tsp baking powder, 25 g/1 oz soft light brown sugar, 50 g/2 oz currants or sultanas, instead of the quantities given above. Add 25 g/1 oz bran when mixing the dry ingredients.

Pumpkin Scones

For these delicious scones, use leftover steamed or baked pumpkin cooked without liquid.

FOOD VALUES	TOTAL	PER PORTION
Protein	36g	3g
Carbohydrate	233g	19g
Fat	36g	3g
Fibre	11g	1g
kcals	1338	112

fat for greasing
300 *g*/11 *oz well-drained cooked pumpkin*
25 *g*/1 *oz butter, softened*
15 *ml*/1 *tbsp caster sugar*
15 *ml*/1 *tbsp golden syrup or honey*
1 *egg, beaten*
250 *g*/9 *oz self-raising flour*
pinch of salt
2.5 *ml*/½ *tsp ground cinnamon*
1.25 *ml*/¼ *tsp grated nutmeg*
50-125 *ml*/2-4 *fl oz milk*

Grease a baking sheet. Set the oven at 230°C/450°F/gas 8. Mash the pumpkin.

Mix the butter with the sugar and syrup or honey in a bowl. Mix the egg with the pumpkin. Add to the butter and sugar, mixing thoroughly. Sift the flour, salt and spices into a bowl, then fold into the pumpkin mixture, alternately with 50 ml/2 fl oz milk. Add extra milk, if required, to make a soft but not sticky scone dough.

Knead the dough lightly and pat it out to 2 cm/¾ inch thick. Cut into rounds with a 5 cm/2 inch cutter. Put the scones on the prepared baking sheet. Bake for 12-15 minutes, until golden brown.

MAKES 12

Tea Brack

'Brac' is a Celtic word for bread. The dried fruits in this teabread are soaked overnight in tea to flavour and plump them up.

FOOD VALUES	TOTAL	PER PORTION
Protein	97g	2g
Carbohydrate	1605g	33g
Fat	30g	1g
Fibre	36g	1g
kcals	6675	139

fat for greasing
500 *g*/18 *oz sultanas*
500 *g*/18 *oz seedless raisins*
500 *g*/18 *oz soft light brown sugar*
750 *ml*/1 ¼ *pints black tea*
3 *eggs, beaten*
500 *g*/18 *oz plain flour*
5 *ml*/1 *tsp baking powder*
15 *ml*/1 *tbsp ground mixed spice (optional)*
honey for glazing

Soak the dried fruit and sugar in the tea overnight. Next day, grease three 20 × 10 × 7.5 cm/8 × 4 × 3 inch loaf tins. Set the oven at 150°C/300°F/gas 2.

Add the eggs to the tea mixture, alternately with the flour in three equal parts. Stir in the baking powder and spice, if used. Turn the mixture into the prepared loaf tins.

Bake for 1½ hours, or until the loaves sound hollow when removed from the tins and tapped underneath. Leave to cool. Melt the honey and brush it on the cooled loaves to glaze them.

MAKES 3 LOAVES

NUTRITION NOTE

The food values per portion are based on each loaf yielding 16 slices, each about 1 cm/½ inch thick. Half wholemeal flour may be used with white flour to increase the fibre content of the loaf.

Fatless Fruit Loaf

FOOD VALUES	TOTAL	PER PORTION
Protein	42g	4g
Carbohydrate	588g	49g
Fat	11g	1g
Fibre	16g	1g
kcals	2473	206

fat for greasing
300 *g/11 oz mixed dried fruit*
150 *g/5 oz dark Barbados sugar*
200 *ml/7 fl oz strong hot tea*
1 *egg, beaten*
300 *g/11 oz self-raising flour*

Put the fruit and sugar in a large bowl. Pour the hot tea over them. Cover and leave overnight.

Next day, line and grease a 20 × 13 × 7.5 cm/8 × 5 × 3 inch loaf tin. Set the oven at 180°C/350°F/gas 4. Stir the egg into the tea mixture. Stir in the flour and mix well. Put the mixture into the prepared loaf tin.

Bake for 1½ hours. Cool on a wire rack. When cold, wrap in foil and store in a tin.

MAKES ABOUT 12 SLICES

MRS BEETON'S TIP

Vary the flavour of this fruit loaf by using different varieties of tea. As well as the lightly flavoured types, such as Earl Grey, try some of the stronger fruit teas and spiced teas.

Date or Raisin Bread

FOOD VALUES	TOTAL	PER PORTION
Protein	35g	3g
Carbohydrate	321g	27g
Fat	68g	6g
Fibre	12g	1g
kcals	1957	163

fat for greasing
200 *g/7 oz plain flour*
15 *ml/1 tbsp baking powder*
5 *ml/1 tsp salt*
large pinch of bicarbonate of soda
100 *g/4 oz dates or seedless raisins*
50 *g/2 oz walnuts or almonds, whole or chopped*
25 *g/1 oz lard*
50 *g/2 oz black treacle*
50 *g/2 oz dark Barbados sugar*
150 *ml/¼ pint milk*

Grease a 20 × 13 × 7.5 cm/8 × 5 × 3 inch loaf tin. Set the oven at 180°C/350°F/gas 4. Sift the flour, baking powder, salt and bicarbonate of soda into a large bowl. Chop the fruit and nuts finely if necessary, and add them to the dry ingredients.

Warm the lard, treacle, sugar and milk together in a saucepan. The sugar should dissolve, but do not overheat it. Add the liquid to the dry ingredients, then mix to a stiff batter. Pour into the prepared loaf tin.

Bake for 1½ hours. Cool on a wire rack. When cold, wrap in foil and store for 24 hours before cutting.

MAKES ABOUT 12 SLICES

Banana Bread

The riper the bananas used for this popular teabread the more flavoursome will be the result.

FOOD VALUES	TOTAL	PER PORTION
Protein	54g	5g
Carbohydrate	400g	33g
Fat	85g	7g
Fibre	12g	1g
kcals	2485	207

at for greasing
300 g/11 oz plain flour
inch of salt
5 ml/1 tsp bicarbonate of soda
75 g/3 oz margarine
100 g/4 oz granulated sugar
3 eggs, beaten
3 ripe bananas
15 ml/1 tbsp lemon juice

Grease a 23 × 13 × 7.5 cm/9 × 5 × 3 inch loaf tin. Set the oven at 190°C/375°F/gas 5. Sift the flour, salt and bicarbonate of soda together.

Cream the margarine and sugar in a bowl. Beat in the eggs. Mash the bananas with the lemon juice. Add to the creamed mixture, then work in the dry ingredients. Put the mixture into the prepared tin.

Bake for 50-60 minutes, until golden brown. Cool on a wire rack.

MAKES ABOUT 12 SLICES

Oatmeal Gingerbread

FOOD VALUES	TOTAL	PER PORTION
Protein	31g	1g
Carbohydrate	216g	10g
Fat	61g	3g
Fibre	10g	–
kcals	1480	70

fat for greasing
100 *g/4 oz plain flour*
1.25 *ml/¼ tsp salt*
15 *ml/1 tbsp ground ginger*
5 *ml/1 tsp bicarbonate of soda*
100 *g/4 oz fine oatmeal*
50 *g/2 oz butter or margarine*
50 *g/2 oz soft light brown sugar*
20 *ml/4 tsp black treacle*
1 *egg*
75 *ml/5 tbsp milk or soured milk*

Line and grease a 18 cm/7 inch square tin. Set the oven at 180°C/350°F/gas 4. Sift the flour, salt, ginger and bicarbonate of soda into a mixing bowl. Add the oatmeal. Heat the butter or margarine with the sugar and treacle gently in a saucepan until the fat has melted.

In a bowl, beat the egg and milk together. Add the melted mixture to the dry ingredients with the beaten egg and milk mixture. Stir well. Pour into the prepared tin and bake for 1-1¼ hours until cooked through and firm to the touch. Cool on a wire rack.

MAKES ONE 18 CM/7 INCH CAKE

NUTRITION NOTE

The food values per portion for the gingerbread are based on the cake yielding 21 pieces. The values given for the Soda Cake (right), are calculated on the cake providing 16 slices and they do not include butter for spreading. Remember that the cakes or teabreads do not have to be eaten in one go as most freeze well. Cut the cake into squares and wrap these individually before freezing for a ready supply of lunchbox or after-school treats.

Soda Cake

This plain loaf cake of Mrs Beeton's day is similar to a teabread. Serve it thickly sliced and buttered.

FOOD VALUES	TOTAL	PER PORTION
Protein	41g	3g
Carbohydrate	351g	22g
Fat	60g	4g
Fibre	9g	1g
kcals	2024	127

225 g/8 oz plain flour
50 g/2 oz butter or margarine
100 g/4 oz currants
100 g/4 oz moist brown sugar
2 eggs, beaten
2.5 ml/½ tsp bicarbonate of soda
75 ml/3 fl oz milk

Base-line and grease a 900 g/2 lb loaf tin. Set the oven at 190°C/375°F/gas 5.

Sift the flour into a bowl, then rub in the butter. Stir in the currants and sugar and make a well in the middle of the mixture. Pour in the eggs. Stir the bicarbonate of soda into the milk, then pour the mixture over the eggs and mix lightly. Gradually work in the dry ingredients and beat well.

Spoon the mixture into the prepared tin, then level the surface. Bake for 45 minutes. Cover the top of the cake loosely with a piece of foil, keeping the oven door open for the shortest possible time. Continue to cook for a further 15 minutes, or until a skewer inserted into the centre of the loaf comes out clean. Cool on a wire rack.

MAKES ONE 900 G/2 LB LOAF

Lunch Cake

If making this with children in view you may wish to reduce the amount of spice.

FOOD VALUES	TOTAL	PER PORTION
Protein	41g	4g
Carbohydrate	384g	38g
Fat	80g	8g
Fibre	11g	1g
kcals	2326	233

fat for greasing
225 *g/8 oz plain flour*
1.25 *ml/¼ tsp salt*
10 *ml/2 tsp mixed spice*
2.5 *ml/½ tsp ground cloves*
5 *ml/1 tsp ground cinnamon*
5 *ml/1 tsp cream of tartar*
2.5 *ml/½ tsp bicarbonate of soda*
75 *g/3 oz margarine*
100 *g/4 oz sugar*
75 *g/3 oz currants*
50 *g/2 oz seedless raisins*
25 *g/1 oz cut mixed peel*
2 *eggs*
50 *ml/2 fl oz milk*

Line and grease a 15 cm/6 inch round cake tin. Set the oven at 180°C/350°F/gas 4.

Sift the flour, salt, spices, cream of tartar and bicarbonate of soda into a mixing bowl. Rub in the margarine until the mixture resembles fine breadcrumbs. Add the sugar, currants, raisins and mixed peel.

In a bowl beat the eggs lightly with the milk. Make a hollow in the dry ingredients and pour in the milk mixture. Stir, then beat lightly to a soft consistency. Spoon into the prepared tin and bake for 1¼ hours or until cooked through and firm to the touch. Cool on a wire rack.

MAKES ONE 15 CM/6 INCH CAKE

NUTRITION NOTE

The food values per portion for both the Lunch Cake and the Vinegar Cake (right) are based on a yield of ten slices in each case.

Vinegar Cake

FOOD VALUES	TOTAL	PER PORTION
Protein	28g	3g
Carbohydrate	326g	33g
Fat	71g	7g
Fibre	9g	1g
kcals	1977	198

fat for greasing
200 g/7 oz plain flour
1.25 ml/¼ tsp salt
75 g/3 oz margarine
75 g/3 oz soft dark brown sugar
50 g/2 oz currants
50 g/2 oz sultanas
25 g/1 oz cut mixed peel
175 ml/6 fl oz milk
5 ml/1 tsp bicarbonate of soda
15 ml/1 tbsp malt vinegar

Line and grease a 15 cm/6 inch round tin. Set the oven at 180°C/350°F/gas 4.

Mix the flour and salt in a mixing bowl and rub in the margarine until the mixture resembles fine breadcrumbs. Stir in the sugar, dried fruit and peel.

Warm half the milk in a small saucepan. Stir in the bicarbonate of soda until dissolved. Add this with the remaining milk and the vinegar to the dry ingredients and mix thoroughly.

Bake for 1 hour, then reduce the oven temperature to 160°C/325°F/gas 3 and bake for a further 30–40 minutes, or until cooked through and firm to the touch. Cool on a wire rack.

MAKES ONE 15 CM/6 INCH CAKE

Flapjacks

FOOD VALUES	TOTAL	PER PORTION
Protein	12g	1g
Carbohydrate	150g	8g
Fat	50g	3g
Fibre	7g	–
kcals	1061	53

fat for greasing
50 g/2 oz margarine
50 g/2 oz soft light brown sugar
30 ml/2 tbsp golden syrup
100 g/4 oz rolled oats

Grease a 28 × 18 cm/11 × 7 inch baking tin. Set the oven at 160°C/325°F/gas 3. Melt the margarine in a large saucepan. Add the sugar and syrup, and warm gently. Do not boil. Remove from the heat and stir in the oats.

Press into the prepared tin, then bake for 25 minutes or until firm. Cut into fingers while still warm and leave in the tin to cool.

MAKES ABOUT 20

VARIATIONS

Sultana Flapjacks Add 50 g/2 oz sultanas to the basic mixture, stirring them in with the oats.

FOOD VALUES	TOTAL	PER PORTION
Protein	13g	1g
Carbohydrate	185g	9g
Fat	50g	3g
Fibre	8g	–
kcals	1198	60

Honey Flapjacks Use clear honey instead of golden syrup; continue as in the main recipe.

FOOD VALUES	TOTAL	PER PORTION
Protein	12g	1g
Carbohydrate	149g	7g
Fat	50g	3g
Fibre	7g	–
kcals	1057	53

Sesame Flapjacks Sesame seeds contribute their own, distinctive flavour to this traditional recipe. Press the flapjack mixture into the tin, then sprinkle a layer of sesame seeds over the top and press them down well with the back of a spoon. Do not use roasted sesame seeds.

FOOD VALUES	TOTAL	PER PORTION
Protein	14g	1g
Carbohydrate	151g	8g
Fat	59g	3g
Fibre	8g	–
kcals	1150	58

Anzacs

These Australian specialities became popular during World War One, when they were often sent to the Anzacs – soldiers of the Australian and New Zealand Army Corps.

FOOD VALUES	TOTAL	PER PORTION
Protein	21g	1g
Carbohydrate	304g	8g
Fat	121g	3g
Fibre	15g	–
kcals	2315	64

fat for greasing
75 *g*/3 *oz rolled oats*
100 *g*/4 *oz plain flour*
150 *g*/5 *oz sugar*
50 *g*/2 *oz desiccated coconut*
100 *g*/4 *oz butter*
15 *ml*/1 *tbsp golden syrup*
7.5 *ml*/1½ *tsp bicarbonate of soda*

Grease two baking sheets. Set the oven at 160°C/325°F/gas 3. Mix the rolled oats, flour, sugar and coconut in a bowl. In a saucepan, melt the butter and syrup gently. Meanwhile put 30 ml/2 tbsp boiling water in a small bowl, add the bicarbonate of soda and stir until dissolved. Add to the melted mixture and stir into the dry ingredients.

Spoon scant tablespoons of the mixture on to the prepared baking sheets, leaving plenty of space between them. Bake for 20 minutes. Cool on the baking sheets.

MAKES ABOUT 36

Buns

These small buns may be baked in paper cases or greased patty tins if preferred, in which case the consistency should be softer than when the buns are put on a baking sheet. The mixture should drop off the spoon with a slight shake, so increase the egg and milk mixture to about 150 ml/¼ pint. If baked in patty tins, the mixture will make 14 to 16 buns.

FOOD VALUES	TOTAL	PER BUN (12)
Protein	27g	2g
Carbohydrate	231g	19g
Fat	72g	6g
Fibre	6g	1g
kcals	1638	137

fat for greasing
200 g/7 oz self-raising flour
1.25 ml/¼ tsp salt
75 g/3 oz margarine
75 g/3 oz sugar
1 egg
milk (see method)

Thoroughly grease two baking sheets. Set the oven at 200°C/400°F/gas 6.

Sift the flour and salt into a mixing bowl. Rub in the margarine until the mixture resembles fine breadcrumbs. Stir in the sugar. Put the egg into a measuring jug and add enough milk to make up to 125 ml/4 fl oz. Add the liquid to the dry ingredients and mix with a fork to a sticky stiff mixture that will support the fork.

Divide the mixture into 12-14 portions. Form into rocky heaps on the prepared baking sheets, allowing about 2 cm/¾ inch between each for spreading. Bake for 15-20 minutes or until each bun is firm to the touch on the base. Cool on a wire rack.

MAKES 12 TO 14

MRS BEETON'S TIP

Plain flour may be used for the buns, in which case add 10 ml/2 tsp baking powder, sifting it with the flour.

VARIATIONS

Chocolate Buns Add 50 g/2 oz cocoa to the flour and 5 ml/1 tsp vanilla essence with the milk.

FOOD VALUES	TOTAL	PER PORTION
Protein	37g	3g
Carbohydrate	237g	20g
Fat	83g	7g
Fibre	12g	1g
kcals	1794	150

Coconut Buns Add 75 g/3 oz desiccated coconut with the flour and an extra 10 ml/2 tsp milk.

FOOD VALUES	TOTAL	PER PORTION
Protein	32g	3g
Carbohydrate	239g	20g
Fat	119g	10g
Fibre	16g	1g
kcals	2097	175

Fruit Buns Add 75 g/3 oz mixed dried fruit with the sugar.

FOOD VALUES	TOTAL	PER PORTION
Protein	29g	2g
Carbohydrate	285g	24g
Fat	73g	6g
Fibre	8g	1g
kcals	1839	153

Seed Buns Add 15 ml/1 tbsp caraway seeds with the sugar. Food values as for main recipe.

Walnut Orange Buns Add the grated rind of 1 orange to the flour. Stir in 100 g/4 oz finely chopped walnuts with the sugar.

FOOD VALUES	TOTAL	PER PORTION
Protein	42g	4g
Carbohydrate	237g	20g
Fat	141g	12g
Fibre	10g	1g
kcals	2326	194

Old English Cider Cake

FOOD VALUES	TOTAL	PER PORTION
Protein	36g	3g
Carbohydrate	284g	24g
Fat	97g	8g
Fibre	7g	1g
kcals	2122	177

fat for greasing
225 *g/8 oz plain flour*
7.5 *ml/1½ tsp grated nutmeg*
1.25 *ml/¼ tsp ground cinnamon*
5 *ml/1 tsp baking powder*
pinch of salt
100 *g/4 oz butter or margarine*
100 *g/4 oz caster sugar*
2 *eggs*
125 *ml/4 fl oz dry still cider*

Line and lightly grease a shallow 20 cm/8 inch square cake tin. Set the oven at 180°C/350°F/gas 4.

Sift the flour into a bowl with the spices, baking powder and salt. Cream the butter or margarine with the sugar until light and fluffy, then beat in the eggs. Beat half the flour mixture into the creamed mixture. Beat in half the cider. Repeat, using the remaining flour and cider.

Spoon the mixture into the prepared tin and bake for 50-55 minutes until the cake is cooked through and firm to the touch. Cool the cake on a wire rack.

MAKES ONE 20 CM/8 INCH CAKE

MRS BEETON'S TIP

A nutmeg grater is an invaluable accessory, but is difficult to clean. A child's toothbrush, kept specifically for the purpose, is ideal.

FROZEN TEA-TIME TREATS

BAKED ITEMS FREEZING CHART			
Type of cake, pastry or bread	**Preparation for freezing**	**High quality storage life**	**Thawing/baking instructions**
Biscuits	Form dough into 2 cm/¾ inch diameter roll. Wrap. **Note** Baked biscuits are best stored in tins without freezing.	2 months	Thaw in refrigerator for 4-5 minutes. Cut in slices and bake at 190°C/375°F/gas 5, for 10 minutes.
Bread	Pack in polythene bags. Crusty bread quickly loses its crispness in the freezer.	1 month	Thaw at room temperature for 4 hours.
Cakes (uniced)	Cool completely and wrap.	4 months	Thaw at room temperature for 2-3 hours.
Cheesecakes	Make baked or refrigerated variety in cake tin with removable base. Open freeze and pack in rigid container. Types relying on gelatine for texture and shape are best avoided as they become very soft on thawing.	1 month	Thaw for 8 hours in refrigerator.
Crumpets and muffins	Pack in polythene bags.	1 month	Thaw in wrappings at room temperature for 30 minutes before toasting.
Fruit pies	Brush bottom crust with egg white to prevent sogginess: **1)** Bake, cool, and pack.	**1)** 4 months	**1)** Thaw to serve cold, or reheat from frozen for 20 minutes at 200°C/400°F/gas 5, then 15-20 minutes at 190°C/375°F/gas 6.
	2) Use uncooked fruit and pastry, open freeze, and pack.	**2)** 2 months	**2)** Bake from frozen at 200°C/400°F/gas 6 for 30 minutes, then at 190°C/375°F/gas 5 for 30-40 minutes.
Sandwiches	Do not remove crusts. Spread with butter or margarine. Do not use salad fillings, mayonnaise or hard-boiled eggs. Separate sandwiches with interleaving film and pack in foil or polythene.	1 month	Thaw at room temperature and remove crusts, or toast under grill while still frozen.
Scones	Pack in small quantities.	2 months	Thaw at room temperature for 1 hour. Bake frozen scones at 180°C/350°F/gas 4 for 10 minutes.

INDEX